Caring for someone with an alcohol problem

Mike Ward

AGE Concern

© 1998 Mike Ward
Published by Age Concern England
1268 London Road
London SW16 4ER

First published 1998

Editor Caroline Hartnell
Production Vinnette Marshall
Designed and typeset by GreenGate Publishing Services, Tonbridge, Kent
Printed in Great Britain by Bell & Bain Ltd, Glasgow

A catalogue record for this book is available from the British Library

ISBN 0-86242-227-2

Bulk orders

Age Concern England is pleased to offer customised editions of all its titles to UK companies, institutions or other organisations wishing to make a bulk purchase. For further information, please contact the Publishing Department at the address on this page. Tel: 0181-679 8000. Fax: 0181-679 6069. E-mail: addisom@ace.org.uk.

Contents

About the author

Mike Ward is currently Assistant Commissioning Manager (Mental Health/Alcohol and Drug Services) for Surrey Social Services. He has worked in the field of substance misuse since leaving the University of Kent in 1980. He was founder and director of Surrey Alcohol and Drug Advisory Service. He was a member of the Age Concern/Alcohol Concern working party on alcohol and older people. He has written extensively on this and related subjects.

Introduction

'I have lived with my husband John for 22 years. For 18 of those years I have also lived with his alcohol problem. When John finally decided to get some help for his drinking I was absolutely over the moon, but after a while I noticed that all the attention was focused on him. He was getting all the help; he was being cared for and getting all the praise for what he'd done. Friends would come up and tell me how proud I must be about the efforts he was making. I was left with this voice screaming in my head "what about me?" I had put up with his abominable behaviour for 18 years while he was out drinking and having fun. No one had offered me any help. Now here he was having all the attention and praise lavished on him. I feel guilty for saying it, but I felt rather left out in the cold.'

Ruth

'I live with my two children, my husband, Steve, and his 73-year-old mother, Anne. She is widowed and has lived with us for three years. However, this relationship is gradually breaking down because of her drinking. She has been drinking heavily since the death of her husband four years ago and is now drinking a quarter of a bottle of spirits per day. As a result she is not taking care of herself and is no longer going out and this is putting a huge strain on myself, Steve and the kids. There have even been violent scenes, and I think that Steve may have hit his mother in the past. Steve is very keen that she goes into some kind of facility to receive help. Our home environment is not really suitable for her to come off alcohol. She tried to stop drinking 15 months ago but only managed to do it for about two weeks. She has also had contact with the local Community Alcohol Team, but since she does not want to do anything about her drinking they have been unable to help her. She has been to her doctor because of the depression she has experienced since the bereavement and he has prescribed her an anti-depressant. I no longer know what to do, I am at my wits' end.'

'None of us drinks alcohol. We drink delicious, liberating, inspiring or socially significant liquids which happen to contain alcohol.' This is the view of Jancis Robinson, the respected wine pundit. Others have called alcohol evil, sinful or demonic. Whatever we may call this substance, we in the UK spend over £25 billion each year on buying alcoholic drinks – the largest expenditure on any item after food and housing.

Alcohol is a central part of our culture. It has always had huge religious significance. It is central to the sacraments of the Christian Church, condemned and outlawed by Islam. In literature, it makes itself felt everywhere from the plays of Shakespeare to the latest episode of the most popular soap operas. Just as significantly, in the view of some commentators, it provides almost three-quarters of a million people with their livelihood and provides a significant part of our visible exports to the world. Alcohol is both a drink and more than a drink.

As long as there has been alcohol, there have been alcohol problems. In the Bible, Noah's sons found their father in a very drunken state; Roman histories are full of alcohol-induced debauchery; Macbeth's Porter rails drunkenly against the effects of alcohol on his sexual desire; Hogarth drew its savage effects on society in his cartoon of Gin Lane; and the nineteenth-century temperance movement stirred passions about alcohol to a fever pitch. Despite this alcohol can still be regarded, in some ways, as a hidden problem.

Newspapers have made us familiar with the alcohol problems of footballers, television personalities and politicians, but many people still seem able to ignore alcohol problems among their own acquaintances. 'He drinks quite a bit but he's not an alcoholic or anything!' is a common enough comment. This apparent blindness is particularly marked when it comes to older people.

'Is it really a problem for older people?' an apparently amazed young journalist asked this author on one occasion, as if it was scarcely credible that people over 65 years of age could drink, let alone have problems. Those who do recognise that some older people drink heavily often regard it as a foible or an eccentricity rather than a cause for concern. Even senior professionals and policy-makers in the caring professions, such as politicians, civil servants and directors or managers of social services departments, seem to find it hard to believe either that older people have alcohol problems or that this is an issue worthy of much attention. Yet talk to anyone who works with older people on a daily basis and the stories of alcohol problems are legion.

Alcohol is both our favourite drug and the forgotten drug. More people drink alcohol than smoke, gamble or use illegal drugs. Each year thousands of people will die prematurely because of their misuse of alcohol. Every week people will be killed or seriously injured by others in drink-related accidents. Every day children will be emotionally and physically abused by parents under the influence of alcohol. The statistics are almost overwhelming.

Yet, because alcohol is so familiar, if not well loved, it is easily ignored. Far more attention is paid to the dangers of illegal drugs than to the effects of alcohol. The tragic death of a teenager under the influence of Ecstasy attracts much greater attention in the newspapers than the far more common deaths of teenagers under the influence of alcohol. The lonely death of a heroin user found frozen in a railway station lavatory seems to elicit more attention than the equally appalling death of a homeless street drinker. This is not the place to attempt to either explain or criticise that imbalance. The purpose of this book is to highlight the ways in which those, like Sarah and Ruth above, who are concerned – or, more importantly, directly affected – can tackle the problems caused by alcohol.

In the last few years there have been some steps in the right direction. The Government's strategy for health, 'The Health of the Nation', has at last begun to recognise the contribution of alcohol to a whole range of health problems from coronary heart disease to mental illness. As a result it has set a target of reducing the number of men drinking more than 21 units of alcohol per week from 28 per cent in 1990 to 18 per cent in 2005, and the number of women drinking over 14 units per week from 11 per cent in 1990 to 7 per cent in 2005. These are challenging targets, and if they are to be met there will need to be as many resources put into fighting alcohol misuse as there have, into tackling drug misuse. More effort will have to be put into health education, taxes on alcohol will need to rise, and treatment services will need to be improved.

Such major political initiatives are vital, but this book tackles the issue not from the strategic national viewpoint of the Department of Health but from the far more personal and practical standpoint of the Sarahs and Ruths of this world – those people who live with the problem on a daily basis. If alcohol is the forgotten problem, then the needs of those who care for the problem drinker are even more concealed. This book will address the very special needs of those who care for someone with an alcohol problem.

Alcohol problems are not limited to any one group in society. Women as well as men, Asians as well as Europeans, the old as well as the young – all are susceptible to alcohol. Thus, although it gives particular emphasis to the problems of caring for an older problem drinker, much of this book will be relevant to anyone who is caring for a problem drinker. There is no need to justify the emphasis on older people – they deserve attention as much as problem-drinking teenagers or their parents. However, those who are reading this book because of a concern about a younger drinker should be assured that most of what is said is relevant to every age group.

A note on the words we use

Numerous words exist to describe a person with an alcohol problem; some of them are confusing, some are plain abusive. This book will use the phrases 'alcohol problem', 'drink problem', 'problem drinker' and 'a person with a drinking problem'. The main alternatives are 'alcoholism' and 'alcoholic'. These have been rejected both as conjuring up a very negative picture and as being somewhat misleading. Those who are interested in this choice of word will find more details in Chapter 1.

One of the difficult tasks facing any author is the decision on which personal pronoun to use throughout the text. Tradition used to dictate that 'he' was the preferred choice. However, not only is this generally sexist, but in a book about older people it is also inaccurate. The majority of people over 65 are women and the text should reflect that situation. Thus faced with the choice between the often ungrammatical 'they' or the clumsy 'he/she', this author has decided to redress the ancient imbalance and use the pronoun 'she' throughout, unless the context dictates otherwise.

1 Describing the problem

This chapter gives you the key facts about alcohol and the effects that it can have on people. It covers important information about the alcoholic strength of different drinks and introduces the 'unit of alcohol' – a standard measure for the alcohol content of drinks. It looks at the drinking and driving laws and discusses how much people – particularly older people – can drink before endangering their health.

The chapter then goes on to discuss what we mean by an alcohol problem and how we recognise that someone has one. It provides important information about the physical, social and psychological effects of alcohol. The chapter concludes by considering how many people, of all ages, have alcohol problems.

Laura

'I am at my wits' end to know how to tackle the problem. I feel so alone, living with someone who is now always drunkenly depressed and morose.'

'My husband Jack is 72, 19 years my senior, and has been drinking heavily most of his life, and certainly since I met him through a dating agency 21 years ago. I came from a heavy-drinking family; both my father and grandfather died of liver cirrhosis and my younger brother, Tom, became

1

addicted to heroin in the 1960s and spent 15 years kicking the habit. With such a background, I had always promised myself that I would never drink and certainly never marry a drinker.

'When I met Jack, he was already widowed, but he had his own successful business and a stable lifestyle; he seemed very different from most of the other men I had met. However, his business meant a great deal of socialising and consequently drinking. So, although I rarely saw Jack drunk, I began to realise that he drank most lunchtimes and evenings. As a result, he was often tired and morose in the evenings after work. I disliked this side of him, but when I spoke to Jack about it he just brushed it aside.

'I finally realised the seriousness of the situation five years into our marriage when Jack was arrested for drink-driving and was found to be four times over the legal limit. He lost his licence, but being his own boss he was able to manage the situation so that the punishment was more of an irritation than a serious problem.

'So you can imagine how relieved I was when, at the age of 60, Jack sold the business and retired. For two blissful years, Jack drank much less and we had a reasonably happy life. We took a number of exotic holidays. However, at the Christmas after his sixty-second birthday, Jack slipped on a patch of ice; he fractured his hip and injured his back very badly. He was laid up for a long time, and perhaps because of his boredom and frustration he began to drink heavily again.

'Jack has never recovered full mobility after the accident and finds walking very difficult now. He commonly spends the day at home drinking alone. I am at my wits' end to know how to tackle the problem. Money is not the issue and, I must say, Jack is never aggressive towards me. It is simply that I feel so alone, living with someone who is now always drunkenly depressed and morose.'

Deirdre

'My friends tell me that I am mad to bother with him, and that it would be better to leave him to stand on his own two feet.'

'I am 79 now, an age at which I feel I deserve to have a rest from looking after people. I am widowed with only one daughter, Sheila, who now sadly lives in Australia. However, my only grandchild, Martin, aged 27, lives only a mile away and in my view is a "raving alcoholic".

'My daughter, Sheila, had a troubled childhood, but she married when she was 30 and moved to Australia with her new husband and our grandson, Martin. This appeared to help Sheila, and from all accounts she has been relatively stable since the move down under. Arthur, my husband, died five years ago and Sheila and Martin, now 22, returned for the funeral and then decided to stay on for a couple of months. It was during this time that Sheila told me that Arthur had abused her as a child. It was a devastating blow, made worse by the fact that Sheila made it clear that she hated my house, with all its memories and associations, and loathed England generally, and had no intention of coming back to live here again.

'However, I was somewhat comforted to learn that Martin had found a job locally and had decided to stay in a bedsit on the other side of town. This pleasure turned into a nightmare. Martin quickly lost the job, apparently because he was drunk at work, and subsided into a state of continual drunkenness. At first I couldn't understand how he funded his drinking, but then he started visiting me and demanding loans and when I didn't help him he would simply steal things. The trouble is I don't have the heart to say anything to him – I would prefer to have him visiting on those terms rather than not to see him at all.

'The problem is that the demands on me have increased in recent months. As the police have begun to pick Martin up for drunkenness, my name is always given as the nearest relative. On a couple of occasions I have been called to the police station in the early hours of a Saturday morning. My friends tell me that I am mad to bother with him, and that it would be better if I left him to stand on his own two feet. Yet somehow I can't abandon him – to be honest I almost feel I owe it to him.'

How much do you drink?

If you were asked 'How much alcohol did you drink last week?' would you be able to answer. If not, you would not be alone; many of us have difficulty in giving an accurate answer. So, you might be interested in how much alcohol is contained in these liquids we love so well and spend so much money on. It can be surprisingly difficult to discover this. Take a look at the following case study:

Frank and Susie

Frank finished work on Friday evening and stopped for a drink – a pint of lager – on the way home. Later that evening, he went to his local and had two more pints of lager, a bottle of Tennents Extra and a single whisky. On Saturday he and his girlfriend Susie went out to dinner. They had a Martini beforehand, a bottle of wine between them and a liqueur each to finish. Susie drove home. On the Sunday lunchtime, they went out and had a half of lager each.

Now ask yourself the following questions:

- How much alcohol did Frank drink over the weekend?
- How much alcohol did Susie drink over the weekend?
- Was Susie over the legal limit when she drove home on Saturday?
- What was Frank's blood alcohol level at the end of Friday night?
- What would it have been on the Saturday morning when he woke up?

This is not a GCSE examination. As you read down this page you may be tempted to ignore the challenge, but these are vital questions. Anyone who drinks alcohol, in whatever form, needs to be able to answer them if they are to avoid drink-driving convictions, physical harm and other alcohol-related problems. Have a think about the questions and then read on to see if you have answered them correctly.

A unit of alcohol

As the case study shows, the great variety of drinks and the varying quantities in which alcohol is served make it very difficult to determine exactly how much has been consumed. In order to make sense of this profusion of drinks, it is necessary to have one single measure against which we can judge the strength of drinks.

This measure is a **unit of alcohol**. All the questions about comparative strengths of drinks can be readily answered if each drink is understood in terms of the number of units of alcohol it contains. One unit of alcohol is equivalent to:

- one pub measure of spirits;
- half a pint of ordinary beer;
- one small glass of wine;
- one small glass of sherry.

From this simple information, we can tell that Frank's lagers on the Friday night amounted to six units and to this was added another unit in the guise of the single whisky. On the Sunday Frank and Susie each had one unit in the form of their halves of lager.

However, alcohol is by no means always consumed in pubs. Measures of spirits and wines poured at home, for instance, are almost always much larger than those served in pubs and bars. Moreover, some lagers and strong beers – often sold in cans and bottles – may contain far more alcohol than ordinary beer, and some lager can be four times as strong. From the information given on bottles and cans, it can be very difficult to know how much alcohol they contain.

So Frank's seven units consumed on Friday evening were significantly increased by the strong lager, which could have had as much as three units in the single can that he drank. Susie and Frank's Saturday drinking is also difficult to calculate.

- Were their Martinis exact unit measures or were they more generous home servings containing two or three units?
- How big was the bottle of wine – 75cl or a full litre? What strength was the wine – was it a white wine with relatively

small amounts of alcohol, say 8%, or a full-bodied red with over 12% alcohol?

■ Which particular liqueur did they have?

The more detailed list of unit values in the section below gives more information.

As can be seen, it is very difficult to determine exactly how many units Susie and Frank drank on Saturday night, because the quantities are vague, but it is likely that they had at least six units each (two each in the martini, three in the wine and at least one each in the liqueur).

Detailed information on unit values

Technically speaking every 8 grams of alcohol in a drink counts as one unit. Unfortunately, drinks come in all shapes and sizes and it can be very difficult to determine exactly how many units are in each serving. The situation has improved in the last few years. In the past the alcoholic strength of beers was measured in terms of 'specific gravity' and the strength of spirits by 'degrees proof'. Nowadays all drinks are labelled with the percentage of alcohol. Thus a bottle of whisky will be 40% alcohol, while an ordinary-strength beer will be just over 3% alcohol. The information below fills in some other important information.

There are about:

■ 30 units in a 75cl bottle of spirits;
■ 7–9 units in a 75cl bottle of table wine;
■ 13 units in a 75cl bottle of sherry.

Most beers are in the region of 3–4% alcohol, eg Carlsberg Pilsner, Castlemaine XXXX and Red Stripe (half pint = 1 unit at 3–4% alcohol by volume).

But some beers can be much stronger:

- Half a pint of Fosters Export, Holsten Pils, Kronenbourg 1664 or Tennents Extra will contain 1½ units (5–6% alcohol by volume).
- Half a pint of Carlsberg Special Brew, Kestrel Super or Tennents Super will contain 2½ units (8–10% alcohol by volume).
- Gold Label is higher even than these at 10.9% alcohol by volume.
- Ciders and perrys tend to be in the region of 5–8% alcohol by volume.

Low and no-alcohol drinks

There are some beers, lagers and wines now on the market which contain only small amounts of alcohol. These are a useful addition to the range of alternatives available to non-drinkers or those wishing to avoid driving while over the limit. However, it is important to note that they fall into two distinct groups:

- Alcohol-free drinks must contain less than 0.05% alcohol by volume.
- Low-alcohol drinks should not contain more than 1.2% alcohol by volume.

While the former are essentially the same as a glass of lemonade in terms of their alcohol content, low-alcohol drinks do contain a noticeable amount of alcohol. If someone has been drinking during the evening, switching to these drinks as an alternative may still increase their blood alcohol levels.

Mixing drinks

Contrary to popular belief, mixing drinks is no more harmful than drinking one type of drink – as far as the effects of the alcohol are concerned. What counts is simply how much alcohol is in the drink. It is, of course, perfectly possible that a particular drink or combination of drinks might disagree with someone for some other reason – just as certain foods may disagree with a person.

Drinking and driving

The other question that Frank and Susie need to address is whether they drove while over the legal limit at any point. This is an important matter, but unfortunately a rather complicated and uncertain calculation. On the one hand, it depends on a very straightforward measurement of the amount of alcohol in the body. This can be measured by testing breath, blood or urine. Nowadays the police talk about the legal limit in terms of 35 micrograms of alcohol per 100 millilitres of breath. However, most people are more familiar with the limit in terms of 80milligrams of alcohol being present in 100 millilitres of blood. Both equate to the same level of alcohol consumption.

This limit is very clear cut. What is less certain is how many drinks will be required to raise a particular individual's blood alcohol level to the legal limit. On average it will take:

- 4–5 units to raise a man's blood alcohol level to the legal limit;
- 3–4 units to raise a woman's blood alcohol level to the legal limit.

This will vary greatly from person to person. The larger a person is, the more drinks it will take to reach that limit. Thus, on average, men can drink more than women, simply because women are likely to be smaller. The other factor influencing this equation is how long the body takes to break down a unit of alcohol. On average the body will eliminate one unit of alcohol every hour, but again this varies greatly from individual to individual: some individuals will break a unit of alcohol down in just half an hour, others will take over two hours to achieve the same result. Women, whatever their size, will always be able to drink less alcohol than men before reaching the legal limit because women's bodies break alcohol down more slowly than men's.

So was Susie over the limit when she drove on Saturday night after drinking? She had consumed six units, which would certainly have taken her over the legal limit, and in the time they were out she may have eliminated only three units. Thus, she was dangerously close to the legal limit.

These are the plain facts about the legal limits. There are many arguments for reducing the legal limit, but this is not the place to rehearse them. The much simpler message ought to be that, no matter what the legal limit, research has shown that it is much safer not to drink and drive at all. Even small amounts of alcohol can slow reaction times, impair concentration and change the way in which the users respond to light, and this makes driving a more risky process.

How much is it safe to drink?

Susie and Frank also need to consider whether the quantities they are drinking are going to cause more problems in the longer term as well as their very immediate concerns about drinking and driving. Will, for example, Susie's drinking endanger her health if she drinks at that level week after week? In order to help people determine how much they can drink and still stay healthy, the Health Education Authority and some of the Royal Medical Colleges met in the early 1980s and agreed 'sensible drinking limits'. These recommended that:

- Men should drink no more than 21 units of alcohol per week.
- Women should drink no more than 14 units of alcohol per week.

It was also recommended that this drinking should be spread out over the week, with two or three drink-free days each week. It is not safe or healthy to drink all 21 or 14 units on a Saturday night and then abstain for the rest of the week.

New sensible drinking limits

In the 1990s the Government began to face pressure to review these guidelines. This pressure came particularly from the drinks industry, which felt that the advice was too restrictive, especially in the light of evidence about the beneficial effects of low levels of alcohol consumption on the heart. A committee was set up to consider this question. When its conclusions were finally reported in

9

December 1995, they confirmed the evidence about the beneficial effect on the heart of small amounts of alcohol and gave muted support for the idea of revising the benchmarks for safe drinking to:

- 3–4 units a day for men;
- 2–3 units a day for women.

This advice was supported by the Government and represents official Department of Health policy. However, there has been much dissent from this view from the Royal Medical Colleges and those working with problem drinkers. This book can only observe that if effective limits of 28 units and 21 units per week are sensible, then 21 units and 14 units are even more sensible. Above all, it should be noted that this guidance relates only to the health effects of alcohol: a person may well experience social problems at much lower levels of drinking, for example a conviction for drinking and driving.

While physical health is the main reason for controlling alcohol consumption, it is worth remembering that a person's mental health can also be affected. If a person is depressed, alcohol will worsen the depression and should therefore be avoided. If someone is on mood-altering drugs, then alcohol should only be consumed after consulting a doctor or pharmacist. However, the most obvious problem is simply that people with poor memory may well lose count of the quantity drunk, thus losing control and worsening their condition.

How much should older people drink?

Contrary to popular wisdom, there is no reason why a person should accept lower sensible limits simply because they slip past a particular landmark birthday. People do not lose their ability to process alcohol as they blow out the candles on their sixty-fifth, seventieth or even eightieth birthday cake. People's ability to cope with a particular level of alcohol consumption is related to their physical condition, not their age. There are many younger people whose physical condition will mean that they can safely or sensibly drink far less than their contemporaries.

The key influences on an individual's safe limit are:

- their physical health;
- their weight;
- whether they are on any medication;
- the state of their liver.

An underweight person who is on some sort of medication because of poor physical health should observe a lower safe limit than a more healthy contemporary, no matter what their age. Conversely, a healthy and hearty 69-year-old may be able to drink just as much as a younger person. However, it is true that in general as people grow older their livers will become less able to break down alcohol. Thus, some doctors have suggested that as a general rule older people should set themselves a lower limit, perhaps between a third and a half lower than the general limits. This book endorses that advice.

What is an alcohol problem?

Jenny

'Evelina is 79 years old and lives next door to me. She moved here about ten years ago after her previous house became too much for her. At first she was a wonderful neighbour but in the last couple of years her drunkenness has caused problems to all her neighbours. She can be heard shouting and banging about at odd hours. She often knocks me up when she's had too much and on occasions she will stand out in the street and shout at passers-by. I guess that she is now totally drunk for three days each week. I am really worried that she is going to hurt herself or even someone else one of these days.'

Two of the commonest questions asked about alcohol problems are

- How do I recognise them?
- How many people with alcohol problems are there in the UK?

11

If we are to identify those people who need help with their drinking, we must have an understandable definition of the problem. Unfortunately, defining the problem is not as easy as it might at first appear. In this century alone, experts have moved from regarding such problems as a sign of moral weakness, to regarding them as a medical condition or illness; more recently, they have been viewed as social problems or pieces of learned behaviour.

You will often have heard people being described as 'alcoholics'. It is a term that is both widely used and widely misused. Many people assume that 'alcoholism' is a clearly defined medical condition which doctors can apply to a person in the same way that they might diagnose measles. This is not the case. There is no agreed definition of the term 'alcoholic'.

The traditional idea of alcoholism as a disease argues that 'alcoholics' experience loss of control over drinking and, once started, are unable to stop drinking. The difficulty is that it is very difficult to prove that someone has lost control. Many drinkers who appear hopelessly out of control will argue that they are perfectly in command of the situation but have simply chosen to get drunk. More significantly, there is a whole group of drinkers who drink in 'binges'. These drinkers may go without drinking for very long periods of time and then, for no apparent reason, set out on a chaotic binge. These people have not lost control totally but only temporarily. The following case studies highlight these problems.

Alistair

Alistair is a retired and wealthy bachelor. He lives alone apart from a married couple who act as his cook and his chauffeur. He starts each day with a couple of double whiskys, drinks a bottle of burgundy with his lunch, has two sherries before dinner and another bottle of wine with the meal, and finishes the day with a double brandy. His doctor told him that he was slowly killing himself. He told the doctor he didn't give a damn about his health and hasn't been back since.

Timothy and Susan

Timothy is 21, unemployed, and married with a seven-month-old daughter. His only source of income is State benefits. Timothy spends most evenings at home but likes to go down to a nearby pub every lunchtime and have a couple of pints with another unemployed friend. Susan, his wife, is very upset that Tim is spending nearly £20 a week on alcohol.

Carlton

Carlton went to the pub on Saturday lunchtime and had four pints of lager. Afterwards he and some friends took several cans back home to watch some videos. Later they went to another pub, played some pool and drank more lager. In the evening they went on to a party. Just as he was leaving, Carlton lost his balance and fell down the stairs, knocking himself out. He woke up in hospital with head injuries.

Frances

Frances is 19. She recently got a good job as a computer rep. She was especially pleased, as a smart car went with the job. The day she got the job she went out to a club with some friends to celebrate. When they left the club there were no taxis to be found. Frances thought she would take a chance and drive home. 'This is the last time I'll be using this old banger,' she thought. The police stopped Frances before she had got half way home. She was fined. She also lost her driving licence and, of course, her new job.

So which one is the 'alcoholic'? The public image of the alcoholic is of a person who drinks very heavily almost all the time or, at the very least, drinks in wild binges and then recovers for a period before having a further binge. Only Alistair and possibly Carlton fit this image but, ironically, Alistair is experiencing the fewest problems. He is wealthy and doesn't care about his health. He doesn't drive and he doesn't have a family scrutinising his drinking. On the other hand, Timothy and Frances would probably not be regarded as alcoholics, yet they both have very immediate problems caused by their drinking. Timothy is placing his wife and children under an almost intolerable financial burden by spending a very large proportion of the family income on alcohol. Frances has imperilled her career by drinking and driving.

The popular image of alcoholism tends to obscure the wide range of people who have problems because of alcohol but do not necessarily drink every day. Moreover, alcoholism is often used as a term of abuse, which is in itself a problem. People who have serious drinking problems are not going to be very happy about being labelled alcoholic. This may even be a deterrent to their seeking help.

As a result of these problems the World Health Organisation abandoned the term 'alcoholism' and now talks about 'alcohol dependence syndrome'. This is a much broader and more all-encompassing definition, but the word 'syndrome' is a little medical for some people's liking.

As a result most people working with problem drinkers have given up asking the question 'Is he an alcoholic?' or 'Are there signs of the alcohol dependence syndrome?' and now find it much more useful to ask the following questions:

■ Has this man got a problem related to his drinking?
■ Is this woman experiencing any harm because of her drinking?

If you look again at the case studies, you can see that Alistair, Timothy, Susan, Carlton and Frances are all suffering some form of harm because of drinking. However, not all of them would necessarily regard it as a problem. If you said to Carlton 'You're an alcoholic!' he could happily deny it and you would never be able to prove the contrary. However, if you pointed out the specific harm drinking had caused, you would be on much more solid ground.

This approach is particularly relevant to many older people. Because of their physical health, financial circumstances or other factors, many older people may not drink particularly large quantities of alcohol, but these smaller quantities may still be regarded as a problem. Take a look at this case study:

Celia

Celia is an 86-year-old woman living in her own home. She has been widowed since she was 73 and has lost contact with the few friends that she had. As a result, at first no one realised that she was beginning to fall and injure herself on a regular basis, because she tends to ignore any but the most serious injury. However, after a particularly serious accident in which she fractured her wrist, her doctor undertook a thorough assessment of her situation. He discovered that Celia had begun to 'top up' the waning effects of her sleeping pills by drinking a couple of whiskys before bedtime. This had affected her movement to such an extent that she was regularly falling on her way to bed.

Celia's drinking alone would scarcely have raised the eyebrows of even the most concerned of family members. What could be the harm in a couple of whiskys? Yet, as we have seen, the use of even small amounts of alcohol by someone who is already vulnerable can have a very harmful effect.

How to recognise that someone has an alcohol problem

As a result of situations such as Celia's, it is impossible to give a simple, snappy definition of an alcohol problem. Instead, we have to decide whether a person is suffering any of a whole range of harms and problems. It is simple and convenient to consider these problems related to alcohol under three separate headings:

15

- social problems;
- physical problems;
- psychological problems.

In reality, of course, people do not experience just one sort of problem. They have various mixtures of these difficulties. Moreover, the problems under each of these headings can have more than one aspect. The alcohol field has developed a useful model for considering the definition of these problems. It clusters all the social, physical and psychological aspects into three groups:

Social, physical and psychological problems related to immediate intoxication This is probably the least acknowledged and most widespread group of alcohol-related problems. You will be well aware of the problems associated with 'football hooligans', 'lager louts' and other such instances of a high level of intoxication. It is important to realise that quite a low level of intoxication can give rise to problems – drinking and driving, minor domestic accidents, disagreements, arguments and hangovers. All of us are exposed to these problems. You do not have to be a drinker. Being jostled by a drunken 'lager lout' is as much an alcohol-related problem as that same lager lout's broken nose obtained in a fight.

Social, physical and psychological problems caused by regular heavy consumption of alcohol Continual excessive consumption of alcohol causes a variety of problems in addition to those related to intoxication. A number of diseases are recognised as particularly alcohol related. These include problems with the liver, such as cirrhosis, fatty liver disease and hepatitis, as well as other diseases such as diabetes, damage to the circulatory system, brain damage, peripheral neuritis, gastritis and cancer of the oesophagus. Regular heavy drinking also gives rise to a range of social, legal and psychological problems.

Social, physical and psychological problems related to dependence on, or addiction to, the drug alcohol This group is by far the best known. Such problems are commonly seen as the problems of 'alcoholics'. It has been estimated that between 1 per cent and 5 per cent of the population may experience problems of this sort.

The following lists look at the social, physical and psychological problems caused by immediate intoxication, long-term heavy use and dependent use of alcohol. These lists will act as a useful indicator of some of the signs and symptoms of alcohol problems.

Social problems related to alcohol

Intoxication

Family arguments
Domestic violence
Child neglect/abuse
Domestic accidents
Absenteeism from work
Accidents at work
Inefficient work
Public drunkenness
Public aggression
Football hooliganism

Criminal damage
Theft
Burglary
Assault
Homicide
Drinking and driving
Taking cars and driving away
Road traffic accidents
Sexually deviant acts
Unwanted pregnancy

Regular heavy consumption

Family problems
Divorce
Homelessness
Work difficulties

Unemployment

Fraud
Debt
Vagrancy
Habitual convictions for drunkenness
Financial difficulties

Dependent use

Many of the problems outlined above, plus:

■ Less and less variation in drinking habits
■ Drinking becoming more important than other aspects of life

Physical problems related to alcohol

Intoxication

Accidents

Acute alcohol poisoning

Cardiac arrythmia	Failure to take prescribed medication
Foetal damage	Gastritis
Gout	Hepatitis
Impotence	Pancreatitis
Strokes	

Regular heavy consumption

Brain damage	Breast cancer
Cancer of mouth, larynx, oesophagus	Cardiomyopathy
Cirrhosis	Diabetes
Fatty liver	Foetal damage
Gastritis	Gout
Hepatitis	Infertility
Liver cancer	Myopathy
Neuropathy	Nutritional deficiencies
Obesity	Pancreatitis
Raised blood pressure	Reactions with other drugs
Sexual dysfunction	Strokes

Dependent use

Many of the problems outlined above, plus:

- Withdrawal symptoms, such as anxiety, discomfort and shaking, owing to the absence of the drug
- Tolerance to alcohol
- Relief drinking – to alleviate withdrawal symptoms
- Return to original drinking patterns after abstinence
- Craving for alcohol

Psychological problems related to alcohol

Intoxication

Amnesia	Anxiety
Attempted suicide	Depression
Insomnia	Suicide

Regular heavy consumption

Amnesia

Attempted suicide

Delirium tremens

Depression

Hallucinations

Misuse of other drugs

Withdrawal fits

Anxiety

Changes in personality, eg aggression

Dementia

Gambling

Insomnia

Suicide

Dependent use

Many of the problems outlined above, plus:

■ Thinking about alcohol to the exclusion of other thoughts

The physical effects of alcohol on older people

While setting out the signs and symptoms of alcohol problems, it is worth noting the specific physical effects of alcohol on older people. In some ways alcohol affects older people in exactly the same way that it affects younger people. However, because older people are likely to be in a poorer physical condition than younger people, some effects are more likely and more marked than others. Three issues in particular are worth highlighting:

Accidents Alcohol impairs coordination, thus creating the risk of accidents. In an older person whose coordination may already be poor the likelihood of accidents is that much greater. In particular, alcohol can exacerbate tremulousness of the hands. Poor concentration due to alcohol can also lead to accidents. It is not uncommon for drunken pedestrians to be killed by cars because they are not sufficiently aware of what the traffic is doing.

Depression Alcohol is not a stimulant; it depresses the central nervous system. As a result drinking can cause or exacerbate an existing state of depression, perhaps due to a loss or bereavement.

Incontinence Alcohol can increase the likelihood of loss of control of bowel and bladder movements.

It is also worth mentioning Korsakoff's syndrome. This is brain damage caused by excessive use of alcohol. It is almost identical in its effects to senile dementia, and medical practitioners may find it hard to tell the two apart in some cases. Those who are concerned about the psychological capacity of an older person need to bear in mind the possibility that an apparent dementia may be alcohol induced.

Misdiagnosis

So far this section has emphasised the various ways of recognising problem drinkers; it has therefore listed many signs and symptoms. It is worth pointing out the opposite danger – too readily assuming that alcohol is the problem. For example, someone found staggering and collapsing in apparent drunkenness on the streets may well be suffering the consequences of hardening of the arteries. If this misdiagnosis is continued it could lead to the patient receiving inappropriate medication, which will only serve to make matters worse

There are a number of medical conditions which may 'mimic' alcohol problems. The most obvious is the hand tremor caused by Parkinson's disease. To confuse this with the tremor caused by withdrawal from alcohol and thereby have the condition misdiagnosed could have very hazardous consequences for the patient. As with all medical conditions, advice should be sought from a doctor before making rash judgements about a person's physical condition.

How many people have alcohol problems?

How many people in this country have an alcohol problem? You will now be able to see that this is as hard to answer as the question about how to define an alcohol problem. The number of people you include in the answer will depend on how you determine who has a problem. If you suggest that anyone drinking over the safe limit has a problem, the answer will be higher than if you include only those people who are physically dependent on alcohol.

We know that approximately 27 per cent of men (6 million) and 13 per cent of women (3.1 million) drink over the old safe limits of 21 and 14 units respectively (1996 figures).

Reliable statistics also suggest that 6 per cent of men (1.3 million) and 2 per cent of women (500,000) drink over the danger limits of 50 and 35 units respectively.

These latter two figures probably give a reasonable picture of the numbers of problem drinkers. Moreover, they confirm the commonly suspected notion that men are more likely to drink heavily and thus develop problems than women. Other studies suggest that at least a million people in the UK have an alcohol problem and that for every one of these million people there will be two or three carers or dependants who are suffering directly because of that drinking.

How many older people have alcohol problems?

If we turn to the question of whether there are significant numbers of problem drinkers among older people, we find a much more confused picture. A number of American researchers seem to have no doubts. In 1991 one American author estimated that 20 per cent of older people had a significant alcohol problem. Three years later another American researcher suggested that alcohol and substance abuse was the third leading health problem among Americans aged 55 years of age or older.

Such evidence appears almost overwhelming – and yet one could ask the same question and give the completely opposite view. Official statistics show that people aged 55 or over drink less than younger people and that people over 65 drink approximately half the quantities consumed by the population as a whole. There is clearly a tendency for alcohol consumption to decline as people get older.

It is very easy to conclude that there is much confusion about the extent of this problem. One study managed to find estimates of the extent of the problem ranging from 2 per cent of the population through to 50 per cent. The determining factor was almost always the nature of the part of the over-55 population that was studied. However, no matter what the statistics tell us, many readers will know personally that alcohol can and does cause problems for a significant number of older people.

2 Who becomes a problem drinker?

This chapter looks at the many reasons why people develop alcohol problems. In particular, it attempts to look at this issue in a way which makes the drinker's behaviour seem more comprehensible. Understanding why people drink is a key to being able to identify the existence of an alcohol problem. The chapter also looks at some of the reasons for drinking that might affect older people in particular.

Alice

'This is a great cause of concern to his neighbours ... However, as Bob is unconcerned by his behaviour, nobody seems able to help him.'

'I live in sheltered accommodation next door to a 72-year-old man called Bob. He can be quite charming but shortly after he arrived here I was awoken one night by the sound of banging and crashing from Bob's room. All night long he was making a terrible din. When one of the other residents asked him to quieten down, she was met with abuse and threats. Since then these outbursts have occurred every two or three weeks. At first the warden and the other residents thought he had some sort of mental illness and a psychiatrist was called to have a look at him. She recognised that Bob's behaviour was because he was binge drinking.

'Apparently, even before he moved in here, Bob had a history of going on binges during which he consumed a great quantity of scotch and then became very aggressive with his neighbours. That was why he was moved here, we now learn. As a result of this drinking his flat has become increasingly squalid. This is a great cause of concern to his neighbours, the warden and his family. However, as Bob is unconcerned by his behaviour, nobody seems able to help him.'

Why do people develop drinking problems?

The previous sections have looked at the external indicators of an alcohol problem, but it is equally important to understand the reasons why people develop alcohol problems or drink in harmful ways. At first sight problem drinkers may seem to be very strange individuals, whose motivation is certainly hidden and probably inexplicable. Above all it is behaviour which may appear very foreign to anyone who has not experienced the full force of an alcohol problem. You may feel that you could never understand why problem drinkers act in the way they do. This is not necessarily the case. As you read this section think of a piece of behaviour you enjoy, which you feel is a bit of an indulgence (like eating chocolates, lying in bed late in the morning, watching a particular soap opera, or whichever habit comes to mind). As you read you will begin to see that there are plenty of parallels between your – hopefully safe – indulgence and the more harmful behaviour of the problem drinker.

The purpose of drinking

In order to understand the motivation of people with alcohol-related problems, you need to bear in mind that drinking alcohol is a form of behaviour like any other – eating chocolates, watching TV; it is not different in kind. All behaviour serves a purpose; people act in a certain way to gain something or to avoid something, and sometimes both together.

Drinking therefore performs various functions in a person's life. These functions can be grouped under the following headings:

Emotional – for example to stop feeling depressed or angry or to feel happier.

Social – for example, to gain confidence or be part of the group or because it's part of the job.
Physical – for example, to relax tension or alleviate withdrawal symptoms.

Each person has a different set of functions that alcohol performs in her life. As long as alcohol performs the intended function and does not have adverse consequences, there is no problem. Drinking becomes a problem when:

- It continues to fulfil the intended functions in the short term but begins to have longer-term adverse consequences: for example, health problems, marriage breakup, financial difficulties.
- It stops fulfilling the functions for which it is consumed: for example, the drinker gets depressed instead of happy, or finds herself being rejected because of her inappropriate behaviour instead of accepted for being a lively and outgoing individual.

A drinker becomes dependent on alcohol when she is unable to do certain things without it. The dependent drinker's tolerance to alcohol necessitates higher and higher levels of consumption to fulfil the same functions, leading to more and more serious problems. It is only by discovering the functions that alcohol performs in a person's life that a carer can help find other ways of serving these purposes and so assist change. Take a look at the story of Joan.

Joan

JOAN is 69 and worked as personal secretary to the chairman of a major British company. Her work was her life and she never married. However, her mother died shortly before her retirement and since then she has lived alone in a flat in a quiet part of Surrey. When she began to drink large quantities of sherry most days of the week, this caused tremendous concern to friends and neighbours, who were worried that one day she would harm herself in some way. However, it did not worry Joan, who was quite happy with her consumption of alcohol.

Joan was not helped by referral to an alcohol service. She could not see the need to talk about her drinking. As far as she was concerned, her drinking was a real pleasure. Her help came from a local clergyman, who helped her talk through the losses of her mother, her job and the status she had had in her job and the lost opportunity to have a family. After some months of help and support, she began to drink less and to play a more active part in the local community.

Such situations are quite common. Although many drinkers will need more intensive and alcohol-focused help to overcome the immediate physical and social problems caused by drink, this case study highlights that underlying the immediate problems there is usually a set of reasons for drinking which need to be addressed.

Why do older people drink?

It would be impossible to list all the potential reasons for drinking. The list would be as long as the list of problem drinkers themselves. However, both research and experience suggest that older people are likely to drink for one of a number of specific reasons. It is important to remember that older problem drinkers are not simply longer-lived versions of younger drinkers. Some will have begun to drink problematically at an early age but many will not start drinking inappropriately until quite late in life, even in their 80s. The reasons for starting to use, or increasing the use of, alcohol may well be specific to age and circumstances. These include:

To kill pain Older people are very often in pain from one or more of a whole variety of disorders, particularly arthritis and rheumatism, and they may be tempted to resort to alcohol for its well-known powers as an anaesthetic.

To help with sleep problems Alcohol is also known as a means of inducing sleep in those suffering from insomnia. It has a soporific effect, especially when mixed with certain other drugs.

To alleviate loneliness and boredom The retired, the housebound and the very old may find themselves bored or lonely for a variety of reasons. Drink can often help to fill gaps in an otherwise empty existence and provide a routine which becomes an all-important part of the day.

To replace meals Some older people may find it physically difficult to prepare meals for themselves. Alcohol is an easily available source of calories. Despite meals on wheels and home care services, many older people still refuse help. The belief that this is 'charity' is still widespread and evokes very powerful feelings of independence.

To cope with loss Older people inevitably suffer more bereavements than younger people. A partner, a relative or a friend may have died recently. Alcohol is a socially acceptable method of coping with these feelings, provided that it is not used for too long after the initial bereavement. Older people may also be grieving over the loss of a job, their status in the community, their health and appearance, their children, their home, a pet, their security or their independence; ultimately they may be fearing the loss of their own life. Through an additional loss, a person may be reminded of, and start to mourn, previous losses. The older person should always be helped to cope with her loss in as constructive a way as possible. This sometimes requires the help of a professional bereavement counsellor.

Because of their former professions Men and women who worked in the licensed trade and men who were in the merchant navy may well have a background of heavy drinking. These jobs are recognised as high-risk occupations in terms of alcohol-related problems. People's drinking may follow similar patterns in old age. Partners of such people may also follow these drinking patterns. Other high-risk professions include journalism and medicine.

Because they have fewer and different constraints in their lives Younger people may find their ability to drink restrained by the demands of a job, a family and a routine. In the older person these restraints may not exist, because they are retired, they live alone, or they are not bound by socially restricting routines.

27

To keep warm Popular myth has it that alcohol keeps people warm and there is some anecdotal evidence that older people might find it easier to drink than to worry about using heating for which they must pay in the future. However, the evidence on this issue is very limited. In fact alcohol may cause hypothermia. A small study in London which looked at the factors contributing to hypothermia showed that alcohol was significant only in those who had been living rough, and in these cases the homeless lifestyle may have been more significant than the drinking. The question of whether alcohol causes hypothermia is therefore unclear, but we can be very certain that alcohol does not help resolve hypothermia, it will not warm people up – it causes the body to lose heat.

Of course younger people could also be under any or all of these pressures. Bereavement, poverty, sleep problems, pain or boredom can be experienced by anyone. What is significant is that it is quite usual for an older person to be under many of these pressures at the same time. Some older people will thus be under great pressure, which could lead to problem drinking and the need for help.

In particular, bereavement is a very real problem and cause of drinking for older people. In the older age group there appear to be two main types of drinker, early onset and late onset. The former are those who have drunk most of their lives and have simply grown older. The other group are those who have started drinking in later life because of some particular stress or problem. The evidence suggests that bereavement is the most significant of these stresses.

3 Facing a crisis

Many carers will first realise that something needs to be done about somebody's drinking when there is a crisis. This may seem like an opportunity to do something positive about the drinking. This chapter acknowledges that crises can present opportunities, but cautions you to be realistic about what can be done in such a situation.

Once you have dealt as best you can with the immediate crisis, your next step may be to seek help for yourself as carer from an alcohol counselling agency and to investigate what sort of help is available to the drinker.

Rosina

'This is the last straw – I have to do something about Frankie's drinking.'

'I am 62 years old and my husband Frankie is the same age; we have been married for almost 30 years. For most of that time Frankie drank heavily but it always seemed to be contained within the work or social setting. He would certainly get drunk from time to time and once even lost his licence, but he was never abusive to me and we always had enough to get by on. However, after he was made redundant seven years ago, he has drunk more and more chaotically. At times he will be drinking first thing in the morning and continue through until night time. It has put a tremendous strain on our relationship. I try not to let Frankie see me in a state, but I can tell you there have been many times when I've been in tears because of his drinking.

'Last night, however, was the worst of all. Frankie didn't come home and didn't let me know what was happening. That was completely out of character. By three in the morning I was ringing around his friends, but none of them knew where he was. Then at four in the morning the police came round to say that Frankie was in hospital after being beaten up by a group of kids. It seem he got into a drunken row with them at a bus stop and they laid into him. When I saw him he was in a terrible state. This is the last straw – I have to do something about Frankie's drinking.'

How much can the carer do?

Alcohol problems do not suddenly spring from nowhere. Most people with alcohol problems will have begun to drink some time before, often many years ago, and then slowly, for various reasons, the problem becomes more and more entrenched. In the same way, the carer will have watched the problem developing over a long time and will have slowly adjusted to these difficult circumstances by making various compromises in the way she lives her life, in order to accommodate the needs of the drinker. Such a situation may continue for many years until some form of crisis emerges which brings the whole problem out into the open.

The crisis may come in any one of a myriad forms; the drinker may assault the carer, the electricity company may finally cut off the supply because of an unpaid bill, the drinker may be arrested for driving under the influence or some other misdemeanor, the physical or mental health of drinker or carer may be put in jeopardy. Whatever the trigger, there is usually some kind of crisis that brings the matter to a head.

In the case study at the start of the chapter it is a beating up which is the 'last straw', and it is easy to understand how Rosina is determined to act now. Many carers will have been in the same situation and many alcohol agencies will have received calls from people whose husband, wife, child or friend has just landed them with a terrible crisis and want to know what should be done now to resolve the drinking problem.

It is always worth 'striking while the iron is hot', as there may be a great deal of motivation and energy to do something in the midst of a crisis, but it is important to be realistic.

To the hard-pressed carer or relative, the promise to stop drinking and immediately seek help from a specialist service must seem a very positive sign. However, such a promise may be worth very little in the morning. You cannot resolve a drink problem while someone is in a state of crisis. Changing a harmful drinking pattern demands long-term work and the drinker must be in a sober, rational state when hard choices can be faced. The key issue is to be clear about the priorities.

First and foremost, it is important to make sure that everybody is safe. Is the drunken person a risk to herself or to others? If she is raging around threatening people, for example, it may be necessary simply to get out of her way and call the police. If she is in danger of hurting herself or of lapsing into some other kind of medical emergency, then an ambulance may need to be called.

Such crises are not the province of specialist alcohol services – they demand the skills and resources of the emergency services. See pages 84–86 for more on how to protect the drinker and others from harm.

Once all danger is passed, the carer may then feel that now is the moment to push the drinker into change. However, this is not something over which the carer has complete control. The drinker may not wish to change. Thus the first step may actually be for the carer to go out and seek some help for herself from an alcohol counselling agency or self-help group. For the carer, simply admitting that there is a problem and she needs help can be a big step forward. Realising that you are not alone and that many other people are experiencing similar problems to yours can also be very helpful. Chapter 6 outlines the kinds of help and services which are available and how they work.

Last, but certainly not least, the drinker should be offered the opportunity to make changes and seek help as soon as she is in a fit state. But remember, no one can make a drinker change: the best the carer can do is encourage her to seek help in the most positive way possible.

Finding out what help is available

The carer should never overlook the simple solution. The reason that a drinker never seeks help for his or her drinking could be simple ignorance of the services available rather than a reluctance to seek help. The public knows little about the services available for problem drinkers. Most people will be unsure about what is involved in changing the way they drink. Many people will have heard of Alcoholics Anonymous but will have only the haziest idea of how it operates and the majority will know little of the other services that are available. This will be particularly true of older people. Community-based alcohol services are a recent development and thus may be unknown to them.

Ignorance may be compounded by irrational beliefs. Drinkers may have all sorts of fears and anxieties.

- Will they be put into a psychiatric hospital?
- Will they lose their present home?
- Will treatment be painful or unpleasant?
- Will they suffer withdrawal symptoms
- Will they have to give up drinking altogether?

Older people in particular may feel that there is a great stigma attached to seeking help for a drink problem. It is the carer's task to demystify these services and to persuade drinkers that help is both readily available and far from unpleasant. It may be particularly important to reassure the drinker about the confidentiality of the services. Older people from ethnic minorities with more negative attitudes to alcohol may need even more reassurance.

Carers could facilitate this process by contacting and visiting local agencies. This would give them both knowledge of the way services work and contacts to whom the drinker can be referred. Local services will welcome such visits. Carers can then explain what services are available and what treatment involves, reassure the drinker that controlled drinking may be an option, and arrange appointments.

So far the message of this chapter has been one of 'realism'. The carer needs to be realistic about what she can achieve. However, one last word of caution is necessary. The fact that the options available in a crisis are limited does not mean that nothing can be done. Too often carers sit back and hope that things will improve. Everybody needs hope but it can be destructive. It is not enough simply to hope that things will change. Carers must make efforts to change what they can change. The rest of this book will highlight the possibilities.

4 Working for change

This chapter looks at how you can help a problem drinker to change her drinking. It begins with the positive message that problem drinkers can change, but emphasises the importance of setting realistic goals. It then suggests various ways to help people change. These range from the 'tough love' approach used by Al-Anon to structured approaches that the drinker can adopt, such as using a drink diary or listing the pros and cons of drinking.

Juliet

'Continued drinking left him with a string of failed relationships, without a job and eventually homeless. As his mother I was in despair.'

'My son Steve started drinking when he was 15. By the time he was 21 he was drinking the equivalent of a bottle of scotch every day. He had already lost his driving licence twice and had had several convictions for drunken assault. The next 15 years were spent in continued drinking, which left him with a string of failed relationships, without a job, and eventually homeless. As his mother I was in despair.

'On his thirty-seventh birthday Steve stepped in front of a car and spent the next four months in hospital. I am still unsure whether it was an accident or an attempt at suicide but either way it saved his life. An astute doctor made the link between his accident and his drinking and he received visits from a local alcohol agency while in hospital. They referred him to a residential "dry house" where he stayed for nine months. There he learnt a whole new way of life and has now managed to stay sober in the community for five years.'

Can problem drinkers change?

While the mass of facts, figures and opinions surrounding alcohol problems may be of interest, the real concern for anyone living with an alcohol problem is 'What can I do to make the drinker change?' The second half of this book takes you through the strategies you can use in order to encourage change.

This chapter starts with a brief, positive message: **change is possible**. There is a common myth that helping people with alcohol problems is a largely fruitless and unrewarding task. Problem drinkers are seen as reluctant to change, and even those who are willing to give up alcohol are thought to face huge odds in forging a new life for themselves.

If this myth is believed to be true about problem drinkers generally, then the beliefs about older problem drinkers are even more defeatist. 'Why should they change, when they have so little to live for?' seems to be a common attitude. 'It's their only pleasure in life, why take it away?' is another view. Even some medical researchers have put forward this view.

These stereotypes are far too bleak. Many people change their drinking in positive ways. For some it is through complete abstinence; for others it is by learning to control their drinking. This is not to say that there is not much hard work and pain involved for many drinkers before they change, but change is both possible and common. Take a look at the story of Steve at the start of this chapter. You may still feel that a good outcome like this is really possible only with younger drinkers. For older drinkers, surprisingly, the picture is even more positive. The best-known American commentator on older people's drinking problems has written that 'there is no evidence that older persons respond less well to interventions. In fact, results from the available studies often report better improvement rates among elderly persons when compared to younger clients.'

It is very likely that the assumption that advanced age will put a person beyond help is nothing more than a self-fulfilling prophecy; older people then receive less active help and the view that they are unable to change is thereby confirmed. Moreover, there is no reason to think that older people need special or separate alcohol treatment services. They seem to benefit just as much from the normal local services that are available.

Ann

'I was amazed at the changes in my sister. Mary is now 79 and her husband died four years ago. Following his death she slowly became more and more withdrawn and at the same time she increased the amount she drank. Her social contacts became fewer and fewer, and her self-care deteriorated. I recognised what was happening and spoke to Mary about the problem. At first, she was very reluctant even to admit that anything was wrong, but eventually she began to open up about her loneliness and her feelings about the loss of her husband. I arranged for her to see her GP, who encouraged her to change her drinking, and at the same time we began to help improve Mary's social contacts. This attention gradually seemed to elicit the desired change and Mary's drinking has now fallen to very low levels.'

Setting realistic goals

Mary's case is clearly a success story; her drinking has reduced to acceptable levels and her behaviour is no longer causing difficulties. There was a problem and now it has been resolved. This appears to be the ideal situation.

However, it is important to recognise that in other cases success may be less absolute. In some situations, there may be a need to rethink what you mean by success. It is very easy to view success as simply being about permanent lifelong abstinence, but this will not always be the case. Take a look at the following case study.

Residential home warden

'Eric Boyle is 81 years old and a resident in the residential home of which I am the warden. He has been dependent on alcohol, mainly spirits and beer, for many years and has had several periods in hospital for treatment. After moving into the home Eric would confine himself to his room, having acquired alcohol in some form. He would not leave his room to eat, and his physical state became very poor. He would not use a commode or toilet outside his room and he would remain unwashed, refusing to change his clothes. At the same time, he became verbally abusive to anyone who approached him. He was able to buy drink as his two daughters gave him money on a regular basis. We attempted to reason with him but without success.

'A meeting was convened with Eric, his daughters and myself. It was eventually possible to make a contract that we controlled his money supply and purchased and issued his drink on an agreed basis. This was also discussed with him and his GP. Eric continued to refuse help but this method of control worked reasonably successfully. There were periods when he was demanding and hostile, and attempted to manipulate the staff and other residents. But the staff succeeded in getting him to eat, wash, take care of his appearance and leave his room. He only occasionally reverted to a state of drunken self-neglect.'

In Eric's case there has been no permanent change. But there has, none the less, been change and improvement, and such success is worth seeking out and acknowledging. It would be easy to feel a failure because Eric has not 'seen the light' and changed completely, but this is still a success.

As a carer you might feel that you would still prefer a permanent change. However, that is not always going to be possible in either the short or the long term. By not recognising and celebrating these smaller but very positive changes you may both undermine the drinker's achievements and set yourself up for permanent disappointment.

As has been said, working with problem drinkers is unpopular, even among trained professionals. The blame for this is usually placed on the drinkers. Problem drinkers are seen as unwilling or unable to change. If any useful work is to be done, we must abandon this idea. If helping problem drinkers is frustrating, that may well be the fault of those attempting to care for them.

The problem is that all too often people set themselves up to fail by setting themselves unrealistic targets. Problem drinkers may have been drinking for many years. They may be drinking for very deep-seated emotional reasons such as bereavement or abuse. In such a situation it is unrealistic to expect change to occur quickly. It may take many months for a person to recognise that alcohol is causing her a problem and it may take even longer to be able to make and sustain a permanent change.

One of the biggest problems for carers is that they become frustrated when change does not occur quickly. The drinking is causing immediate problems, and those close to the drinker will hope that the solutions can be equally immediate.

This is unrealistic The person who holds such a view is bound to be frustrated. It is tempting to wish for a miracle cure, but the truth is that most change takes a long time.

As far as carers are concerned, there is no magic solution to alcohol problems. However, if there is one message that successful carers must learn it is: *know your limits*. It is very easy to become over-involved with people with alcohol problems. In many ways the nature of alcohol problems invites over-involvement. The solution seems so close, so simple. All the person has to do is to stop drinking or drink less. What could be simpler? At times the problem drinker may even express a real desire to give up drinking and the carer can be pulled into offering just a little more help, only to see it all come to nothing. The basic truth is that we are not gods – we cannot force people to change against their will. We can easily set ourselves up to fail by expecting too much too quickly. There is only a certain amount we can do without the drinker's help and cooperation.

What options does the carer have?

Those caring for problem drinkers are in a difficult position. They may well feel that they are constantly banging their heads against a brick wall, and indeed that is often a very good analogy for what is going on. Let us use it to consider what options there are for the carer.

Imagine, for a moment, that you are walking down a road and suddenly you see someone continually bashing her head against a brick wall. What can you do in that situation? The situation is completely imaginary, so you can do anything you like. Consider for a moment what options are open to you:

- You might well choose to ignore the situation and pass on by.
- You could physically drag the person away from the wall.
- You could attempt to reduce the impact of the blows by putting a jacket or coat in the way to cushion the blows.
- You might try persuading or cajoling, soothing words or angry words.
- You might go and call for some other, perhaps more specialist, help.
- You might even in extreme circumstances be so frustrated that you join in yourself.

This scenario may seem absurd and somewhat divorced from reality, but the choices outlined above are exactly the same options that the person caring for a drinker faces. There are only the same limited number of options as in our imaginary exercise.

Ignore it and pass on by Your initial instinct may be to ask how you can possibly ignore a drink problem, but this is a common response. It is very easy to treat the symptoms of drinking such as ill-health, poor hygiene or confused finances while ignoring the root causes. Unfortunately the carer or warden who lives in close or daily proximity to the problem cannot escape so easily from the effects of the drinking – they are there every day not hidden away in somebody else's home. For the carer who lives with the problem drinker ignoring the problem is not a real option.

Try and restrain the person Most carers will try and stop the drinking by denying the person access to alcohol – this is a very common response both in domestic situations and in places such as residential homes. However, it is a very difficult task. How do you safely and effectively stop an adult, even a bed-bound adult, finding alcohol if she wants it? More to the point, do we have the right to restrain someone's drinking? Does she not have the right to drink if she so chooses?

Try and put something soft between the person and the wall to cushion the blow In terms of drinking this means accepting that the drinking is going to carry on but minimising the harm to the drinker by keeping her warm, clean, nourished and safe – in other words, cushioning the effects of the alcohol. This is a common but controversial approach. If someone constantly cleans up after a person, what pressure is there on her to change? Why should someone reduce her drinking if a carer, family member or friend is willing to pick up the pieces? This is not a criticism, simply the reality of the situation.

Try talking or persuading Talking to the person about the drinking or trying to persuade her to stop is inevitably the most used of all these techniques. Its success will vary immensely with the skills of the carer and the readiness of the person to change. The next chapter will look at effective ways of talking to someone about her drinking.

Call for other help Call for other agencies to help deal with the problem. This seems like a sensible option, but in reality there is very little specialist agencies can do other than the things mentioned above. There are no magic tools.

Join in Joining in seems a slightly flippant suggestion but it represents a real problem. Many carers find that the experience of caring for a drinker can turn them to alcohol to relieve the stress.

We will use these categories to frame the range of responses available that we look at later in the chapter. But before we look at these in greater depth, it is important to return to our starting point in this section – setting sensible limits.

If you look at these six options in the hard light of day, it is clear that none of them offers an easy solution to working with problem drinkers. That is because there are no easy answers. If we go into the caring situation imagining that we will be able to bring about change either swiftly or easily, then we are setting ourselves up to fail. Instead we need to take things step by step.

How people change

This gradual approach is helped if you think about how people change. Two American psychologists, Prochaska and Di Clementi, have produced a model which shows how people change. It outlines the stages of change (see p 42) and is applicable to all sorts of changes. This model was developed working with smokers; but it is applicable not just to things like drinking or drug-taking but to any change, whether it be deciding to buy new curtains or deciding to get a divorce.

J O Prochaska and C C Di Clementi suggest that change happens in stages. In the beginning the person is in **pre-contemplation**, unaware that there is anything wrong with the situation or that there is any need to change. People at this stage deny that there is a problem and seem unconcerned about, or even ignorant of, the harm they are causing themselves.

The person making the change must move into **contemplation**. This is a period of ambivalence in which the drinker is beginning to think about the possibility of change. At one moment she may be convinced of the need to change; at others the feeling that everything is all right or that change is impossible returns. It is important to note that many people at this point may seem to others to be still in pre-contemplation. They may appear to believe that everything is all right, but inside a long dialogue may be going on about whether to change.

The person making the change then moves into **action**. The cigarettes are thrown away, the commitment to cut down drinking is made, the diet is started – the change is made. However, this is clearly not the end of the process. There is a need to move swiftly into the next stage. **Maintenance** is the crucial period in which the person still finds it an effort to hold on to the change and avoid returning to the old patterns.

In the end, hopefully, the change is made and the person moves into **termination**. This is the mirror image of pre-contemplation; she again sees no need to change, but this time because the change has been made.

The stages of change

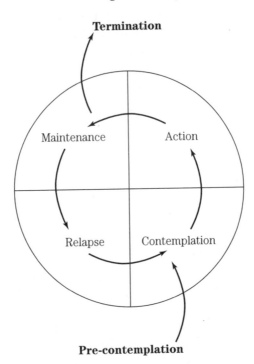

Source: J O Prochaska and C C Di Clementi, 'Towards a Comprehensive Model of Changes' in W Miller and N Heather, *Treating Addictive Behaviours.* Plenum, 1996.

For some, however, they are unable to hold on to the change and they return to drinking heavily, smoking, or whatever. Prochaska and Di Clementi call this **relapse**. From relapse it is very likely that the drinker will return to contemplation.

This model graphically illustrates what has already been said: change is a step-by-step process. Many carers will judge whether they have been successful with a drinker by whether the drinking has stopped. Prochaska and Di Clementi illustrate how this is setting yourself up to fail. The success of efforts made to encourage change will depend on what stage of change the person is at. If a carer has raised the issue of drinking with a drinker who is at the pre-contemplation stage and made her think about the possibility of change, then she has done well. At that point the carer must be prepared to acknowledge that the person will need to spend some time in contemplation before any further change occurs.

This model offers us another positive message. Relapse is part of the process. Drinkers will often not give up in just one attempt. Relapse is not the end of the line; it simply means that the person will need to move around the cycle again.

We will now turn to the options for change. Again it is important to emphasise that none of these options offers an easy answer. The carer who believes that she can change a problem drinker is arguing against sense and setting herself up to fail.

Talking about the problem

Much of this section may seem basic and obvious. It suggests that the best way to talk to a problem drinker is in a calm, rational, adult fashion, when the drinker is sober. Few people would disagree with this. Yet it is easy for frustration to lead a carer to forget it. When someone refuses to acknowledge what seems obvious to everyone else, it is easy for the carer to slip into lecturing, cajoling or trying to persuade the drinker that she ought to change. It is even possible to believe that persuasion is in the best interests of the drinker.

This approach rarely works. It is most likely to lead to resentment and hostility. More frustratingly, the problem drinker may verbally accept what is being said but inwardly reject it and do nothing to change. Let us think about ourselves. You probably dislike being told that you ought to change something about yourself. Are you likely to respond well to such an approach? You might even decide to do more of the thing you are being told to stop out of simple pigheadedness.

If we are to make an impact on people with alcohol problems, we must think very carefully about how we approach them. Let us look at an extreme example: A carer says to her 75-year-old neighbour who is drinking heavily and causing all sorts of problems: *'You ought to give up drinking because you are an alcoholic.'*

This is unlikely to open up a useful dialogue. There are a number of problems with this statement:

- It is an accusation.
- The word 'ought' has moral overtones that are unlikely to be helpful.
- The drinker may find the term 'alcoholic' offensive.
- Using the word 'alcoholic' or even a term like 'drinking problem' can lead the conversation down a blind alley. Both terms are indefinable. The drinker can justifiably argue that she is not an alcoholic because as far as she is concerned alcoholics sit on park benches and drink meths. This kind of dialogue will go nowhere.
- Above all the statement is untrue! The reason the carer is challenging the woman is not because she is an alcoholic but for the much more specific reason that she is causing disruption all around her.

It is much better to talk about your concerns and to be concrete and specific about the effects that alcohol is having on the person. For example; you might say: *'I am worried that the cans of lager you drink are the cause of your recent accidents.'*

This statement is very different. It is much harder to deny because it is talking about you and your concern rather than about the other person. It is about a real situation to which she can readily relate. She is being asked to help resolve the carer's problem. The first statement is a judgement, the second is a statement of the carer's feelings and based on observed behaviour.

There can be no guarantees that even an approach like this will work. But it is more likely to open up a useful conversation than the more accusatory approach.

Using a drink diary

Whether the drinker agrees that it is necessary to change or not, one of the most useful tools for working with someone who needs to change her drinking is a drink diary. A sample 'Personal Drink Diary' page that has been filled in is shown on page 46. At the end of the book you will find a blank diary page; this can be photo-copied for your own use. The diary is used to record:

- how much the person drinks;
- when the drinking occurs;
- where the drinking occurs.

Let us pursue the example of the 75-year-old woman a little further. Even if she does not recognise the need to change, she could be asked to keep a record simply in order to look at how much she is drinking in the most objective way possible. This could be presented as something of a challenge: 'You say you don't drink that much, well let's count how many drinks you have in a week.' Seeing the number of units per day or per week written down in black and white may be an education in itself. Many drinkers have little idea of how much they actually consume, so this may be a way of moving the drinker from the contemplation stage and into action.

The diary will show not only how much alcohol is consumed but also the patterns in the drinking. This may reveal some of the reasons why she is drinking. If the diary is used on a regular basis, it will enable both the drinker and the carer to monitor changes in the drinking.

Of course some drinkers, including some older people, will be unable to complete the diary on their own. In such a case there is no reason why the diary can't be filled in by the carer and the drinker together, and such an activity could lead to a very useful discussion.

Do people lie in diaries? This is a very frequent question. Experience suggests that drinkers tend not to lie; they are far more likely to 'forget' to fill it in. To sit down and forge a diary is quite an admission to yourself that something is wrong.

Finally, the diary itself can be a way of reducing drinking. People who are having to record their drinking find that they are much more conscious of their drinking and may reduce it accordingly.

Personal Drink Diary

Day	Time	Where/ With whom	Type of drink	No of units
Mon	evening	with friends	spirit	6
Tue	evening	with friends	spirit	6
Wed	nothing			0
Thu	lunchtime	alone	beer	4
	evening	at home	wine	4
Fri	evening	at home	wine	6
Sat	lunchtime	at home	wine	6
	evening	at home	wine	6
Sun	lunchtime	at pub	beer	4
	evening	at home	wine	6
			Total units for week	48

Thinking about the effects of drinking

An alternative starting point for a conversation is a 'good and bad things about my drinking' form (again, there is a filled-in sample below and a blank form at the end of the book). This form is a very simple way of weighing up the pros and cons of someone's drinking. It can be used by a drinker entirely on her own and be considered in isolation by her. However, it is best used in conjunction with someone else, either a counsellor or a carer, and used as a springboard to further discussion. This approach has two very useful features. Firstly, it allows the problem drinker to make an objective decision about whether to change or not. The advantages

The good and bad things about my drinking

Good		Bad
Relaxes me	*1*	Hangovers
Become sociable	*2*	Cost
Easier to talk	*3*	Complaints from family
Tastes good	*4*	
	5	
	6	
	7	
	8	
	9	
	10	
	11	

Now ask yourself: do I want to change my drinking?   Yes/No and disadvantages are laid out in black and white and demand that a choice be made. Secondly and perhaps surprisingly, it allows the carer and the older person to see the advantages as well as the disadvantages of continued use. This may at first sight appear perverse. Surely it is in the carer's interest to emphasise the disadvantages and play down any positive aspects?

In reality, it is very important to focus on the advantages of continuing to drink. People do not drink because of the negatives, they drink to gain the positives. If you are to help someone change, you need to recognise what it is that the drinker is gaining by using alcohol. Once this is recognised, alternative strategies can be designed to replace these gains with other, less harmful pleasures.

Doing nothing – 'tough love'

It is perhaps a gross inaccuracy to characterise Al-Anon's 'tough love' approach as 'doing nothing', but it is undoubtedly an approach which emphasises the need to do less rather than more as a way of helping the problem drinker.

The Alcoholics Anonymous (AA) approach to working with problem drinkers has been and still is immensely important and influential in determining how we work with problem drinkers. There is also an organisation called Al-Anon. This is a group for the family members (or 'loved ones') of problem drinkers. Its very existence serves to emphasise the key role played by carers of problem drinkers. Al-Anon recognises both that carers of problem drinkers need a great deal of support to deal with the emotional trauma of living with a drinker and that carers can play a key role in changing the behaviour of the drinker.

The Al-Anon approach to working with family members

This section concentrates on the specific model that Al-Anon uses to help carers do all that they can to change the drinking patterns of the person they care for.

Al-Anon recognises that there may be things that the carer does which, albeit unconsciously, help the drinker to carry on drinking. These could range from the very obvious, such as actually going out and buying the drink, to less obvious support such as scraping together the money to pay bills or providing meals at times which fit with the drinker's drinking pattern rather than when the carer would like to provide them.

Al-Anon argues that in order to help the drinker, the carer must 'disengage' from these activities and stop supporting or colluding with the drinker. This is not easy. It is being cruel to be kind, but it can and does work. Let us take an example.

Sue

'I have been married to Geoff for ten years. Over that time his drinking has become worse and worse. Geoff is a partner in a printing firm and his drinking has put a tremendous strain both on the company's finances and on our relationship. He is occasionally verbally abusive, demands his meals when he comes back from the pub, and often takes our only car out to the pub at weekends, leaving me with the double problem of being anxious about Geoff's drinking and driving and not having a car to take me and the children out. I work part-time and am having to use most of the money to bail out the family's finances, instead of using it to buy the extras I had intended it for. I feel tremendously alone and there seems to be no one that I can turn to or talk to.'

What can Sue do? One can easily imagine that she is at her wits' end, and may come close to a nervous breakdown if she does not receive support and help to resolve her dilemma. How would Al-Anon help Sue?

Simply by attending Al-Anon Sue would be taking a big step forward. She would be admitting that there is a problem and, equally important, recognising that she needs some help to resolve it. The first step towards resolving a problem is almost always admitting that a problem exists. One should never underestimate the difficulty of making that first move. Sue would have been greatly helped if friends or relatives had encouraged her to move forward.

Once at an Al-Anon meeting, Sue would immediately learn a second important lesson. She is not alone. There are at least as many people caring for problem drinkers as there are people with alcohol problems. This obvious fact can be a tremendous comfort to those living with the problem on a daily basis. Even if Sue can draw no other benefit from Al-Anon, this basic support may help her keep on an even keel.

It is to be hoped, however, that she would receive considerably more help. In talking to other members of the group she would learn about their personal situations, and may begin to realise that her situation and her husband's problem are not necessarily hopeless. The prime message that she would receive from Al-Anon is that she is powerless to change her partner's drinking. She is not god, and cannot force someone to change against his will. This sounds immensely depressing; if she cannot change her husband, what can she do? In fact, this idea is very liberating. The key message is that she can begin to think about how she can change what she does in order to improve her lot and perversely also to improve Geoff's situation.

Tough love

As has been said, the approach that Al-Anon uses is 'tough love'. Sue must consider how she is colluding with Geoff's drinking. The first thing she must do is to stop pretending to Geoff that she doesn't mind about the impact his drinking is having on her life. She must make it clear that she objects to not having access to the car, to having her pleasure curtailed to enable her husband to enjoy himself, to having to use her money to plug the hole in the family finances left by his drinking.

In a few situations such openness might make a positive impact by itself, but generally these words will need to be backed up by action. Sue will need to consider ceasing to bail Geoff out financially; if he finds himself in debt, he will need to face the consequences. She could consider providing the meals at a time that suits her, not the pub's opening hours. She could simply take the car at weekends and go out herself. Whatever Sue is doing that helps Geoff's drinking should be stopped. Sue cannot afford to collude with her husband's behaviour.

Although this is very active, it is only the start of the process of 'disengagement', ceasing to do things which make Geoff's life easier. Ultimately this route may lead to much more drastic disengagement. If Geoff still refuses to change, Sue will have to decide her priorities. Would she prefer to stay with a drinking husband or would it be better to leave him and attempt to start a new life away from him?

This is the ultimate stage in disengagement, and facing up to these difficult choices will certainly help Sue improve the quality of her life. For many people such a process may also begin to bring the drinker to his senses. If Sue does nothing to support Geoff any more, his drinking life will become harder and harder, and ultimately he will face the withdrawal of his wife and children. Sue has recognised that she cannot change the drinker; instead she must stop helping him and concentrate on what she can do to change herself.

Many people have found this the best way to change both themselves and the drinker, but it is a course that demands much support and assistance. People in Sue's situation should seek help from advice agencies and groups like Al-Anon.

5 Making the change

Helping someone to reach the point where they are ready to change may seem like the hard part, but there is still much work to be done and some difficult decisions to be made.

This chapter focuses on the work that needs to be done to turn a desire to change into a reality. It is not enough for the drinker simply to want to change; she will need to consider issues such as whether to pursue total abstinence or a form of controlled drinking and how to structure her life in order to minimise the chances of coming into contact with potential drinking situations. This chapter is full of practical advice and some simple exercises that people can do to help think through the necessary changes.

Danielle

'Fortunately, Mum has begun to show signs of improvement ... I can't tell you what a relief it has been to see her change in this way.'

'My mother, Phyllis, is 67, and she moved into a residential home about seven months ago. Despite her being relatively young, I was very relieved when she moved in there. She had to be admitted because she was wheelchair-bound after a stroke and could not return to her top-floor flat, but more than that she simply wasn't coping at home and I couldn't cope with her. Her flat had become very run down and she wasn't caring for herself.

'When she went into the home it was reported by one of the community nurses that she was an "alcoholic". My mother, of course, denied this but it made a lot of sense to me. This will sound silly, but I hadn't realised how much she was drinking and I hadn't made the connection between the way she was behaving and the alcohol. Since Dad died she had got worse and worse; she was forgetful and unkempt and didn't seem to care about her surroundings. In the months prior to the stroke she had started ringing me up at all hours to complain about this or that. It put a terrible strain on both my husband and me.

'After the stroke she appeared to stop drinking. However, after a few months in the home she has begun to pester me and the staff to take her shopping, although what she really wanted was to go to the pub. The staff began to find her drunk in her room on occasions. After some investigations they discovered that she had set up a network of individuals, ranging from more able fellow residents to a long-standing friend who visited her, all of whom brought her small bottles of spirits in ignorance of the other sources of supply.

'The problem became most acute when a cleaner found her slumped drunkenly on the floor of her room in a pool of urine. To their credit the staff called for some more help and she began to receive "counselling" from a key worker.

Fortunately, Mum has begun to show signs of improvement and is now having just one or two drinks at the home's bar when it is opened. She is slowly being rehabilitated to everyday living skills, and it seems likely that the local council are going to offer her warden-assisted accommodation so that she can go back into the community. I can't tell you what a relief it has been to see her change in this way.'

What kind of change should the drinker make?

The first questions to address with the problem drinker are:

- What kind of change should she make?
- Should she attempt to give up drinking completely or should she try controlled drinking?

As a carer you may immediately feel that you have had enough of alcohol and its disastrous effects and would rather that alcohol was abandoned altogether. You may feel that you could never trust the drinker not to go over the top again if she was still drinking even small amounts regularly.

Many people in the alcohol field share this viewpoint. Alcoholics Anonymous believe that lifelong abstinence is the only solution to an alcohol problem. Many doctors and alcohol professionals share this view. In the last 15 to 20 years, however, there has been a growing body of evidence that a sizeable number of problem drinkers can learn to control their drinking. Nowadays many of the mainstream alcohol agencies routinely offer their clients a choice between abstinence and control and have success with both models.

Such evidence may still fail to persuade you that controlled drinking is a good thing. However, to a large extent the decision as to whether someone tries controlled drinking or abstinence is out of your hands. If a person is set on controlled drinking, despite the carer believing that abstinence is the only possible goal, it is surely better to let her try controlled drinking than attempt abstinence unwillingly.

There are also some people for whom abstinence is neither necessary nor appropriate. Many older people whose problem drinking has begun because of a relatively recent crisis such as a bereavement may be able to return to normal drinking without difficulty. Indeed, it is likely that the offer of controlled drinking will be much more of an incentive to change than abstinence. The same argument may also apply to the young who have found themselves having problems with drinking at an early age. Abstinence may be almost a disincentive to change for someone with 50 or 60 years of life ahead of them.

That said, it is important to recognise that some people are more likely to succeed at controlling their drinking than others; for some people abstinence must be the only course. Below is a list of the factors which should influence the choice between abstinence and controlled drinking.

Those more likely to succeed with:

Controlled drinking	Abstinence
Younger people and those with a short history of abuse	Those with a long drinking history
Those in employment	Those without regular employment
Those with a family around them	Those with less support from family and friends
Those suffering less harm – physical, mental and social – from their drinking	Those suffering physical damage, especially liver damage, or psychological harm, eg memory loss
Those not showing signs of physical dependence	Those showing signs of physical dependence
Those in situations, eg jobs, which put pressure on them to drink occasionally	Those who are taking drugs that mix badly with alcohol
Those with lower levels of consumption prior to seeking help	Those who have tried and failed in previous attempts to control drinking

Note This list is neither exhaustive nor exclusive. Just because someone fulfils one of the criteria for one approach, it doesn't mean that she shouldn't try the other approach. However, the more criteria from one column a person matches, the more likely she is to succeed by that method.

The benefits of abstinence

For some people controlled drinking is unadvisable. Those who have liver cirrhosis or other serious medical conditions and those who have experienced severe withdrawal symptoms such as delirium tremens and fits when they have stopped drinking should not be advised to attempt controlled drinking. In all cases it is best to seek medical advice.

Even if someone has chosen to attempt controlled drinking, it is often best to start with a period of abstinence (perhaps 1–3 months) before returning to drink. This will allow the drinker to gain a real sense of self-control before attempting to use alcohol again.

It may help both the drinker and the carer to have an idea of what someone may go through in the days immediately after giving up drinking. When people stop drinking, the body needs time to readjust. Most people can come off alcohol quite safely at home. However, if you or the drinker are ever worried about what is happening or have had a bad experience in the past, a doctor should be consulted immediately. There is no virtue in living through bad withdrawals unnecessarily.

The experience of withdrawal

The first three days tend to be the worst. The drinker can expect to feel anxious, irritable and restless and may even have flu-like symptoms. It is important not to give up at this point – in a week to ten days, these feelings will have passed.

Alcohol has a high sugar content and it is helpful to replace this for the first few days. The best way to do this is by drinking fruit juice. Alcohol also disturbs the natural pattern of sleep. If the drinker can't sleep or wakes after a few hours, do not worry – this is quite normal and will right itself after a few weeks. If she does not already know any, encourage her to learn and use relaxation exercises. There is now a wide range of relaxation aids available.

GPs, health promotion units and health food stores will all be able to help.

As the days go by, the person will find old interests returning. Allow her to enjoy them. Let her watch television as much as she wants but try to encourage her to get some exercise. The drinker should set herself small objectives where she knows she can succeed. Many drinkers decide to give up smoking at the same time that they give up alcohol, but this is going a step too far; it is something that can and should wait until a later date.

The drinker may want to explain to people, especially close friends and relatives, what she is feeling. It will be helpful if these people can be as supportive as possible, but the drinker needs to be prepared not to be upset if they appear to lack faith in her efforts. They, too, need time to readjust.

Stopping drinking in itself will not solve the problems that caused the drinking problem in the first place. After the first week, however, when the drinker is feeling better, both the carer and the drinker will be in a good position to put these into perspective and consider other ways of dealing with them. It is at this time that talking to a counsellor can be especially beneficial.

The drinker must be beware of setting herself up to drink again. Preparations should be made for the moment when someone offers her a drink. What can she do? What will she say? It's not easy to give up alcohol, but by taking one day at a time and being realistic the drinker and the carer can succeed together.

Changing the way someone drinks

If the drinker chooses to pursue controlled drinking, then it will be necessary to look at ways of reducing the amount that is drunk. Below are listed some possible areas for change:

Change the drink This is very simple and very obvious. If the drinker usually drinks pints, cut this down to half pints. If she drinks doubles, ask for singles. Strong lagers or beers can be replaced with ordinary-strength beers; with wines the drinker can go 'continental' and mix water with the wine to reduce the amount of alcohol per glass. It might also be worth trying low-alcohol wine or beer.

Eat while drinking Alcohol's effect is lessened by food, so it is a good idea to eat while drinking. Certainly most people know from experience not to drink on an empty stomach.

Time the drinks Problem drinkers often drink faster than their colleagues, which will contribute to their drinking more. In this situation it is worth setting time limits. The target could be to drink only one pint per hour (or some such limit). Alternatively, a gap – say 20 minutes – might be left between each drink.

Alternate the drinks Instead of sticking to alcoholic drinks all the time, alternate alcoholic drinks with soft drinks. After all, some soft drinks look very similar to alcoholic ones.

Don't gulp drinks It is a good idea to check the way someone drinks. Does she gulp the drinks down quickly? It could be worth consciously slowing down, encouraging the drinker to sip drinks.

Delay the first drink If the drinker has the first drink later in the day, it is almost inevitable that less will be drunk. So if the drinker always takes the first drink at lunchtime, why not delay it until the evening or go out to the pub an hour later than usual.

Don't buy rounds When buying in rounds there is a perceived obligation to have as many drinks as there are people in the round. Moreover, it is often felt that it is harder to choose soft drinks when buying rounds. It is far better to stay out of rounds and buy drinks individually (it could be cheaper too!).

Think about the circumstances of the drinking Some people find that in certain situations, or with certain people, they drink more than at other times. Help the drinker to consider her own consumption and whether there are some people or places that should be avoided?

Making a contract

The most common way of helping people with alcohol problems is through a process of contract-making. The contract may be between a drinker and a carer or between a drinker and a professional helper. Contracts are as applicable to those who are controlling their drinking as to those who have stopped completely.

Contracts do not need to be complicated or threatening. The following is an example of a very simple contract that could be made in any home in the land:

'I told Jim that I was quite happy to cook his evening meal, but that I would not cook it or heat it up at eleven o'clock at night when the pubs had closed. If he was to have his meal he would need to be home at seven o'clock when it suited me to prepare it.'

However, they may also be used in more formal settings:

'In our residential home, if we are concerned that a resident's drinking may be a problem, then our work to do something about that may even begin at the point of assessment. The new resident will be accepted on the basis that she will do such and such about her drinking. However, it may begin at any point. If a resident's drinking is causing a problem, a staff member will sit down with her when she is sober and talk through the situation and set a target, for example only to drink 21 units this week, or to drink no more than two units per day, or not to drink before 7pm or not with certain people, whatever they find helpful or appropriate. These targets can be monitored using a drink diary or some other means of monitoring and a reward may be agreed for meeting the target.

'The question we are asked is "What do we do if the person fails to meet the target?" In ordinary counselling persistent failure to meet targets might lead to the counselling coming to an end. This is not an option for residential home workers. The only course is gentle but continued persistence and the use of such rewards and incentives as are available to the staff. The key is not to give up.'

The following sections provide ideas which can be used in a contract.

Making the change permanent

There is more to resolving an alcohol problem than just changing the amount of alcohol consumed. It is usually necessary to change at least some elements of a person's lifestyle. How much change is needed will depend on how large a part drinking plays in the person's life. For example, if drinking in pubs is a person's entire social life, then finding an alternative lifestyle is going to be essential. This will mean looking at alternative social activities, setting goals in this area, and examining rewards for achieving the target.

This can be taken as the pattern for much of the work that needs to be carried out with the drinker:

■ identifying a problem area;
■ looking at coping strategies or alternatives;
■ setting targets;
■ rewarding the achievement of the target.

The forms on pages 61–62 offer steps towards change. The first helps identify what areas of a person's life need changing. Thus in the sample 'Situations in which I find it hard or easy to avoid drinking' form the person has highlighted being bored and alone as a key reason for drinking. This can be used alongside the Drink Diary and the 'Good and bad things about my drinking' form, which also offer insights into areas for change (see pp 46–47).

The 'What are the alternatives to drinking?' form highlights seeing friends as a better alternative. The 'Targets I will work towards' form shows that joining a local day centre has been set as one of the targets for the coming week. The proposed reward is buying a CD. (Blank forms for photocopying are at the end of the book.)

Goals and rewards are vital. The drinker needs clear targets and the carer needs something to check on. It is therefore important that both goal and reward are realistic and achievable. A goal like 'I want to be nicer next week' is useless because it is unreachable and uncheckable.

Situations in which I find it hard or easy to avoid drinking

Hard to avoid drinking		Easy to avoid drinking
Bored and on my own	1	With husband
At parties	2	When I have something to occupy me
Depressed	3	When I'm happy
	4	
	5	
	6	
	7	
	8	
	9	

Now ask yourself: Can I spend more time in the easy situations and less time in the hard situations?

Targets I will work towards

How many units will I drink this week?

35

What else will I change about my life? (be specific)

I will join a local day centre

How will I reward myself if I reach these targets?

I will buy myself a CD

What are the alternatives to drinking?

---

*In this space write down what alternatives there are to drinking,
what you could do instead of drinking*

Ring up friends and arrange to see them

Ring up children and invite them round

Join a social club

Get more exercise

Now ask yourself: Which of these will I try?

This pattern of goal and reward can continue until both parties are happy with the changed situation.

It is worth returning again to the point that the carer does not have to take on this process. Some situations may be so difficult that outside expertise is essential. There is no failure in asking for help; failure lies in not initiating the process at the very beginning.

Relapse

Most people see a relapse as a disaster, but it is important to remember that it is not the end of the world. If someone drinks again after a commitment to stopping or fails to control her drinking at an agreed level, it is obviously disappointing for both drinker and carer. But it is only a disaster if they choose to see it as such.

If a woman who has been drinking heavily decides to stop and then has a couple of drinks, she can easily become so upset at this 'failure', so guilty, so angry with herself, that this precipitates a far worse drinking episode.

It is important in such a situation that someone points out that things may not be as black as they seem. It could well be that she has drunk less in the last few days than for some considerable time past. Even if this is not the case, she should see that just because she drank yesterday, it doesn't mean that she can't try again. A relapse is not the end of the road, but rather a hiccup along what is undoubtedly a difficult route.

It is equally vital that carers and professionals do not lose heart when someone relapses. If the carer begins to believe that the drinker is really a hopeless case, that will soon be transmitted to her. The carer should realise that there will be ups and downs and that giving up at the first failure is not going to help the drinker.

Nor is relapse necessarily the time to switch treatment plans. The fact that someone has failed to meet an abstinence target does not mean that the target should immediately be switched to controlled drinking. The drinker should stick at a target for a while; only when there has been a fair attempt should alternatives be examined.

On occasions, someone may relapse and have the opposite of the despairing, guilty attitude mentioned. If a problem drinker is minimising the significance of a relapse, then the carer needs to point out that it is quite serious and lead the person back to the start of the whole process.

Relapse is a serious matter, but it is not the end of the world. The carer's task is to help the person look at the drinking episode sensibly – neither as a catastrophe nor as a trifle. Most of all she should be helped to persist in working towards the chosen goal. The 'Why I didn't succeed' form on page 64 offers a way of thinking through the lessons that can be learnt from a relapse. The one certainty is that if nothing is learnt, there will be little scope for avoiding the same problem in the future.

Why I didn't succeed	How I can improve on this next time
I went to a place where I knew alcohol would be available	Avoid gatherings where there is alcohol
I was feeling down at the time	Talk to someone when I'm down
I went with someone who would encourage me to drink	Avoid drinkers

6 What help is available?

Anyone caring for a problem drinker should seek help for themselves, as well as encouraging the drinker to seek help. Although alcohol problems are often kept hidden, there is still a wide range of agencies that people can turn to for help.

This chapter looks at the potential for seeking help from familiar professionals such as a GP and then reviews the range of specialist services that are available. These include Alcoholics Anonymous and other self-help groups, local alcohol advice centres, in-patient units and national organisations such as Alcohol Concern. Most of them will offer help to both the problem drinker and the carer.

Jean

'I know that if I ever had problems again, I'd be ringing them up straight away.'

'The Alcohol Advisory Service was hard to find the first time I went there; it was on the second floor of an office down a side street on the edge of town. But I guess they don't have much money for flash office blocks. I went straight in and was met by a receptionist who immediately introduced me to my counsellor, Diane. It was several weeks before I realised that Diane was a volunteer and not a paid worker. She certainly seemed very expert and appeared to understand my situation.

'She allowed me to talk a great deal in the first couple of weeks, but all the time asking questions to try and understand how and why I drank. I was amazed that she neither told me off nor told me what to do. I suppose I expected it to be a bit like visiting the headmistress. Instead we gradually worked out what changes I wanted to make in my life, how we could make them, and what would stop me moving forward. Each week we would monitor my progress and then explore some of the key issues in greater depth. I never realised that talking could be so tiring or so helpful!

'After about 12 weeks we began to ease off and meet less frequently and a bit later we ended completely, but I know that if I ever had problems again, I'd be ringing them up straight away.'

Non-specialist services

Any professional working in a caring capacity ought to be able to respond positively to someone with a drinking problem. GPs, social workers, other health professionals, personnel staff and employee welfare officers should all have the capacity to recognise such a problem and know what to do when they recognise it. This is not always the case.

Many professionals still appear to be unable or unwilling to recognise alcohol problems; if they do recognise them, they may not know how to respond or respond inappropriately. This leaves the person with the problem and their carer with a dilemma.

This lack of help from mainstream professionals has meant that most people are thrown back on the specialist services as the main source of help. In many ways, however, the best source of help should be those people that already know the person with the problem. This is more likely to be the local GP than an alcohol specialist. Even if they prove unable to provide the type of help that is required in the first instance, they may be a source of longer-term support.

Nancy

'When the social worker who came to see my husband Frank in the hospital heard about his drinking, he simply suggested that he should try and drink a bit less and moved on to another topic. He didn't seem to grasp that I have been trying to get Frank to drink less for ten years and have never managed to get past the first week.'

Community-based alcohol services

John

'The first time I went to the alcohol counselling service I was in a complete mess. I didn't know what to expect and I half expected to see people in white coats.'

Few people know what to expect when seeking help for an alcohol problem. GPs are familiar figures but alcohol agencies are little known, and have at times deliberately tried to hide their identity from passers-by. The general public have no idea how people are helped with an alcohol problem, and the images they do have may be very outdated. Older people in particular may believe that alcohol treatment involves locked wards and invasive psychiatric treatment. Others may recollect hearing about the aversion therapy techniques that were used in the past. These involved attempts to condition the body to reject alcohol by giving people drugs which reacted badly with alcohol and then encouraging them to drink. This technique has largely been abandoned (see p 76 on antabuse).

These days alcohol treatment uses relatively straightforward methods. However, they will vary according to the type of agency that the person attends, and inevitably according to the type and severity of the problems presented by the drinker.

Community Alcohol Teams

Most areas of the country now have local Community Alcohol Teams. (They may also be called Substance Misuse Teams or Drug and Alcohol Teams). These are usually managed by the NHS or social services departments and may either replace or extend local in-patient provision.

These teams will be staffed by a combination of nursing and social work staff with support from psychiatrists and possibly psychologists. Occasionally teams will have additional personnel such as a probation officer, counsellor or alternative therapist such as a specialist in art therapy or shiatsu.

These teams will offer an assessment of a person's needs and may then refer them to other services or provide counselling, groupwork or appropriate medical help such as detoxification. These services will be advertised widely in the local community and information will be available from doctors, libraries, the local Health Authority or the social services department.

These facilities tend to be very informal in their approach. However, an appointment will usually be necessary unless specific drop-in times are advertised; appointments can normally be made by phone. The atmosphere will normally be non-medical and efforts will be made to put people at their ease and to listen to their needs. Any help is likely to be provided at the team offices and will probably consist of weekly or fortnightly counselling and group sessions.

In very large rural areas, the teams may have outposts which are staffed once a week or once a fortnight to provide access to people who cannot travel into the larger centres of population.

Alcohol Advisory Services

Alcohol Advisory Services, which are also known as Alcohol Counselling Services or Councils on Alcohol/Addiction, will appear to the outsider to be very similar to the Community Alcohol Teams. Like the teams, they are based in the community and generally offer both individual counselling and groupwork. The main difference is that they are almost always managed and run by charities and many of their counsellors may be trained volunteers. This does not mean that they are less competent services. There is a long tradition of voluntary work in this field and much of the pioneering work on alcohol services has been led by voluntary bodies. Counsellors are usually trained to very rigorous standards, and many older people value the informal and confidential atmosphere provided by non-statutory agencies. The voluntary agencies are particularly good at offering support to carers. These services can be accessed in the same way as the Community Alcohol Teams, and information about them will be equally available.

It is worth pointing out that these services will usually expect people to attend sober. Other users of the agency will welcome a safe place where it is clear that only sober people will be encountered; and if the agency projects a reasonable but high expectation of clients attending sober, then it is likely that that expectation will be met. Even the most severe drinker is not drunk all the time, and most will turn up sober to see a counsellor without needing to be asked. If a person does turn up drunk, it is not a disaster. The agency will almost certainly make another appointment as soon as possible and ask the person to come sober.

These services will also be confidential, not divulging information about clients except in the most exceptional of circumstances. This may well reassure people, particularly older drinkers.

Self-help groups

Alcoholics Anonymous

Alcoholics Anonymous (AA) offers the oldest and best known of all the treatment options available to problem drinkers. Its success can be measured by the host of imitators from Narcotics Anonymous through to Chocoholics Anonymous. It is impossible to argue with the success of this group. However, it is important to understand how AA works and who it will suit, because a significant number of people do not find that AA's approach suits them.

AA is above all a self-help group. It is a quite phenomenal organisation which has groups in virtually every corner of the world and yet it has no formal leader or even a membership list. It is truly anonymous. Despite that, it has a very strong philosophy regarding the care of people with alcohol problems. AA members believe that 'alcoholism' (as they choose to call it) is a disease characterised by loss of control over drinking. They believe that there are some people who will lose all control over their drinking when they drink even a small amount of alcohol. The only way to handle this problem is thus to admit that you have lost control over drinking and give up drinking completely for the rest of your life.

Admitting this powerlessness in the face of alcohol is the first of AA's Twelve Steps. This is the basic programme through which all AA members seek to pass (the steps are laid out below). To help them through this process, members have two main sources of support.

The first is the regular group meeting. AA is a group process and the core of membership is attending weekly meetings of a local group. Although you may not be readily aware of it, no matter where you live in the UK there is almost certainly a group meeting within a few miles. If you live in one of the large conurbations there will be several meetings available every day. In the early stages of recovery members are encouraged to attend as many meetings as possible: attending 90 meetings in 90 days is a familiar AA recipe for support in the early stages of recovery.

AA'S TWELVE STEPS

AA's approach is best seen in its Twelve Steps, which provide a summary of its approach to recovering from an alcohol problem:

1 We admitted we were powerless over alcohol – that our lives had become unmanageable.
2 Came to believe that a power greater than ourselves could restore us to sanity.
3 Made a decision to turn our will and our lives over to the care of God as we understood Him.
4 Made a searching and fearless moral inventory of ourselves.

5 Admitted to God, to ourselves and to another human being the exact nature of our wrongs.

6 We are entirely ready to have God remove all these defects of character.

7 Humbly asked Him to remove our shortcomings.

8 Made a list of all persons we had harmed and became willing to make amends to them all.

9 Made direct amends to such people wherever possible, except when to do so would injure them or others.

10 Continued to take personal inventory, and when we were wrong, promptly admitted it.

11 Sought through prayer and meditation to improve our conscious contact with God as we understood him, praying only for knowledge of His will for us and the power to carry that out.

12 Having had a spiritual awakening as the result of these steps, we tried to carry this message to alcoholics to practise these principles in our affairs.

Such a list highlights both the structured nature of AA and its spiritual approach to recovery.

The meetings follow a fairly set format: members listen to a keynote speaker talking about recovery or some related theme and then other members follow with their own experiences or testimony. Each speaker prefaces her remarks with the well-known phrase 'My name is XXX and I am an alcoholic ...', which emphasises the member's recognition that she is someone who has lost control over drinking.

The second form of support is the sponsor. Senior members of AA may offer themselves as people whom newer members can contact for support and guidance at any time of the day or night. This is an invaluable source of support and one which other alcohol agencies can never hope to match.

Around this structure is a great deal of supportive literature and tradition which members can draw on for inspiration. Prominent among this material is the so-called 'Big Book', which is a series of members' life stories which can both encourage and act as role models for new and experienced members alike.

Does AA work for everybody?

AA has a long history of excellent work in the alcohol field. However, as has been said, AA is not for everyone. Some people feel uncomfortable with what is perceived as the 'religious' element in AA. AA certainly has a 'spiritual' dimension. The first step demands admitting to a 'higher power' that you are powerless over alcohol. However, even the most cursory examination would suggest that this spiritual dimension is so personalised and so open to individual interpretation that many atheists can slip quite comfortably into the AA approach. Those who complain about the spiritual/religious dimension may well be using that to express other more deep-seated concerns about the group or about their own wish to make changes to their drinking.

That said, there are one or two specific problems which need to be addressed, in particular for older people. The emphasis in AA on group work may deter many people who feel uncomfortable exposing their problems to other people. Older people, already nervous about the stigma of 'alcoholism', may be very resistant to this kind of approach and prefer individual help. This preference is not always in the drinker's best interest. A group approach can be much more helpful, in that the commitment to change will be carefully scrutinised and challenged by other people, and there will be a ready source of advice and help. However, if a person is unwilling to attempt change through a group process, then individual therapy must be the best option.

Equally, total abstinence may not be appropriate for everyone. As already discussed, controlled drinking may well be a good option for people with a relatively short history of drinking problems whose drinking has not caused any dramatic problems. AA will ultimately not be suitable for these people. However, there is no harm in someone who is concerned about her drinking attending a meeting and trying AA for herself. Attending a meeting need not imply a commitment to the AA model of change.

A more practical problem for older people is that the majority of AA meetings are held at night. In larger towns there will probably be daytime meetings, and the many older people who do not like to go out at night can be directed to such meetings. Alternatively, many AA members will be happy to act as a chauffeur for those who would otherwise be unable to attend meetings. For those who are housebound or otherwise unable to travel, for example those in residential homes, AA members may be willing to visit and talk to people on an individual basis.

For those who are not problem drinkers but who would like to learn more about AA, most groups have an open meeting once a month. These enable interested outsiders to gain a glimpse of the workings of AA. For all information about AA there is a single national number which can be called to find the nearest local group (see 'Useful addresses').

Al-Anon Family Groups UK & Eire

Al-Anon offers understanding and support for families and friends of problem drinkers, whether the alcoholic is still drinking or not. Much has already been written above about the philosophy of Al-Anon (see pp 48–51); however, there are a number of points worth highlighting.

Al-Anon is slightly younger than AA but it is still a very well-established organisation with a similarly extensive national and international network of group meetings. It replicates much of the approach of AA. It is a group-based organisation, with a set of Twelve Steps very similar to AA's and its own literature, traditions and support structure. As such, much of what has been said about AA is equally applicable to Al-Anon.

Those who are concerned about a loved one's drinking are always welcome to attend and see if Al-Anon is for them. There are also open meetings for interested parties. The national contact number for Al-Anon is given at the back of the book.

Alateen

It is commonly assumed, from its name, that it is for teenage drinkers; this is not the case. Alateen, a part of Al-Anon, is for young people aged 12–20 who are affected by other people's drinking. This will usually be the drinking of a parent, but could easily be that of a grandparent if the relationship is sufficiently close. Contact Al-Anon for details of Alateen meetings throughout the UK and Eire.

Adult Children of Alcoholics (ACOA)

A separate group, which is not actually part of the AA family but which is very influenced by AA's approach, is Adult Children of Alcoholics (ACOA). This is a much more recent organisation, which was set up to help adults whose childhoods were badly affected by their parents' drinking. Such an experience can lead to emotional problems in later life, and this group seeks to offer support to such people.

In-patient treatment

In-patient alcohol treatment units began to be set up in the late 1950s and early 1960s, reaching the peak of their significance in the 1970s.

Alcohol treatment units are usually separate in-patient units located in psychiatric hospitals. The first such units were run as part of the NHS, but in more recent times there has been an increase in the number of units run by private or voluntary organisations. All these units tend to offer in-patient detoxification followed by a short (6–8 week) residential course; the course will centre on groupwork, with additional individual counselling from a nominated keyworker. The groupwork focuses on such issues as the life history and drinking pattern of the participants, the development of new social skills, and the learning of techniques such as relaxation and assertiveness.

In the past older people may have found it hard to gain admission to NHS in-patient units. As places were limited, older people may have been seen as a lower priority by some units. However, no such bar existed or exists in the private and voluntary sector, although places here will need to be funded either by the client herself or by funding from health or social services.

The most important point to recognise today is that NHS in-patient units are becoming much scarcer resources. As part of the general trend towards community care, the services provided by many in-patient units have been moved into community-based services offering detoxification in a person's home along with a daytime programme of counselling and/or group therapy.

These services can be of great value to people with alcohol problems of any age. It should not be assumed that because a service does not involve some form of 'hospitalisation' it is therefore less valuable. There are many problems with in-patient units, not least the difficulty of moving from the safety of the unit back to the community, so community options may be better in the long run.

Other sources of help

Services for homeless people, women and people from ethnic minorities

There are a number of other specialist services for people with drink problems. For homeless drinkers there is a network of day centres and dry houses. These tend to be appropriate only for those whose drinking problems are very extensive and have caused considerable problems. By and large these houses are used by the younger and middle-aged groups. Older people, who have statutory rights to housing, may neither feel the need to use such facilities nor wish to forsake their privacy to live with a number of other people.

There is also a growing number of specialist services for women and people from ethnic minorities who have drinking problems. At present these tend to be concentrated in larger centres of population. However, if these are of interest it could be worth asking one of the national organisations on alcohol misuse, listed at the end of the book, for information. Even if you are not in the immediate vicinity of the service, these specialist facilities may be willing to offer some help over the telephone.

Telephone helplines

There is now a national helpline for people with alcohol problems called Drinkline. This can provide a great deal of useful help anonymously to people who feel unwilling to talk to someone face to face. Details of this service are provided at the back of the book.

Antabuse

It is worth pointing out the existence of the drug antabuse. This drug is used with a small but significant number of drinkers who are attempting abstinence. It is usually taken on a daily basis (although a longer-lasting implant is also available); if the user then drinks even a small quantity of alcohol, there will be a violent physical reaction.

To many carers, this will sound like a dream drug – a substance which stops someone becoming drunk. Unfortunately, it is not as simple as that. The first issue is that the person has to be willing to take the drug on a daily basis and, of course, not to drink on top of it. The second concern is that many people feel that taking antabuse prevents the drinker from working on the underlying issues which make her drink and developing strategies for avoiding alcohol in the future. Anyone considering the use of antabuse must, of course, consult a doctor for advice.

Health education advice

So far this brief review of alcohol services has concentrated on treatment services. However, you may require simple health education advice. Many of the agencies listed above, especially those based in the community, will be able to supply both information and educational materials. It may also be worth contacting your local health education unit, which will be able to provide relevant materials. You can find the number for your local unit through your Health Authority.

National agencies

There are a number of national organisations involved in work with problem drinkers and their carers. These range from the

Portman Group, an agency sponsored by the drinks industry which produces educational materials and supports research, to the Medical Council on Alcoholism which, as its name suggests, is involved very heavily with the medical care of problem drinkers. However, the main national organisation is Alcohol Concern, the national agency on alcohol misuse.

All these organisations will have a varied range of information about alcohol issues, but Alcohol Concern is the best first port of call for general information. In particular, they have a range of leaflets about alcohol problems as well as a library which provides a wide range of information about alcohol. The addresses of these organisations are at the back of the book.

7 Caring for someone who does not want to change

Not every problem drinker will decide to change once confronted with the problems caused by alcohol. Many carers find themselves looking after or living with someone who doesn't want to change. What can they do?

This section offers help and advice on how to deal with this difficult and stressful situation. The focus of the work is on the long-term management of the problem. Mention is made of how to tackle the short-term crisis of a single drunken incident, but this is not the main focus of the chapter.

One issue is whether to buy alcohol for the person or whether to try and prevent her having any alcohol at all. For those who care for an older drinker in a residential home, the options are different again, and the chapter considers the use of licensed bars in homes.

The final part of the chapter looks at ways of minimising harm and handling a very drunk person.

Winston

'When I ask Dad himself, he just says, "Let me alone, I'm happy as I am."'

'My 75-year-old father has a lovely ground-floor flat that the council gave him after Mum died. Unfortunately, he has become virtually a prisoner in his own home. His problems are clearly due to his long history of abusive drinking. When I was a boy I can remember seeing Dad going down to a nearby social club every night and then hearing him come home and rowing with Mum.

'I guess we all thought that the drinking would kill him, but he outlived Mum who, in my opinion, was worn out by the stress of looking after Dad. I then hoped he would grow out of his drinking as he got older, but nothing changed. And now, even though he finds it very difficult to get out to the off-licence or pub, he is still getting hold of his bottle of scotch.

'Until recently his only source of alcohol was his home carer. One day she decided, after consultation with her manager, that they should no longer buy Dad his usual two bottles of scotch a week. In desperation, he took to leaning out of his window, waving a ten-pound note at passers-by and asking them to buy him a bottle of scotch. Occasionally he was rewarded with a bottle, sometimes he never saw the money again, and on one occasion a young man came into the house, beat him up and took the rest of his money. I am at a loss to know what to do about it. When I ask Dad himself, he just says, "Let me alone. I'm happy as I am!"'

The right to control

Sheila

'I am a community nurse and one of my clients, George, lives in a local authority residential home for older people. He sits in his room and drinks continuously. He can often be heard shouting; he recently had a bad fall, resulting in a cut head. He has an ulcer on his left foot, which I have to dress, and suffers diarrhoea and various stomach problems. I have tried to talk to him about why he drinks. At times he says he is depressed about his life and regrets never marrying. At other times he says "It's a free country" and "Drink is the only happiness left to me". The staff in the home have sometimes had to stop him drinking.'

With a drinker who appears unwilling to change, we are forced to address not only practical issues but also some very complicated ethical issues. For example, do we have the right to control someone's drinking? Do carers have the right to refuse to buy alcohol for people that they think have an alcohol problem? Can a residential home which is trying to offer residents a home-like environment reconcile this with restraining a resident's drinking?

These questions contain a very obvious bias towards the problems posed by older drinkers. The reason for this is quite simple. It is virtually impossible to restrain a younger adult's drinking. You cannot successfully lock a 45-year-old man in his bedroom for any length of time. You cannot stop a 25-year-old woman going down to the shop and buying a drink. It is only with the less physically able, such as those who are largely housebound, that we have any power to control alcohol consumption.

It may, therefore, be possible to restrict a disabled 75-year-old's access to alcohol. We can prevent relatives and friends from bringing it to the house and make other arrangements to prevent its availability. The question is – should we?

Many social services departments are now publishing charters of rights for the residents of their residential homes for older people. One charter, typical of many, has declared 19 such rights, including:

- ■ the right to personal independence, personal choice and personal responsibility for actions;
- ■ the right to the same access to facilities and services in the community as any other citizen;
- ■ the right to expect management and staff to accept where appropriate the risks associated with encouragement of personal independence.

There is nothing apparently exceptional about these rights. They are the rights that we would all expect to have, and would imagine would be applicable to all older people, whether they live in their own home, a family member's home or a residential home. How, then, can controlling someone's drinking be reconciled with these rights?

The answer must be that if the drinking does not interfere with anyone else, then there can be no justification for controlling it. However, other people also have rights. Neighbours, carers and other family members have the right to expect that they will not be unreasonably upset by someone else's behaviour. The charter quoted above thus adds a section about responsibilities: 'No one has complete freedom to do as they please – we all have to take account of the needs of others.'

This book cannot give an answer to this ethical dilemma. Each person must weigh up the issues in the particular circumstances they face. These dilemmas are particularly acute for carers facing the decision about whether to buy alcohol or not and for those who have the power to determine whether or not to allow someone to have alcohol at all. Both of these situations are likely to apply only to those caring for people who have limited mobility.

Do you buy alcohol for a problem drinker?

With most healthy people it is an irrelevant question, but for the less mobile the supply of alcohol will depend on others. Do they have a right to alcohol? Some people would say that people quite clearly have a right to alcohol if they want it and that carers should buy it for them. It is a question that both home care organisations and people running residential and nursing homes face daily.

A recent study showed that people in these organisations have mixed views. Some were very positive about the clients' right to alcohol:

'Yes, we would buy alcohol for our residents. Why not? Who are we to refuse them?'

Others were more restrained:

'We would buy alcohol. We are able to do so because we monitor the supply. How much we would buy would depend on the resident and their behaviour when under the influence of alcohol. Usually finances will decide the limit, but it does depend on the resident's tolerance to alcohol, effective monitoring and cooperation from the resident.'

'Alcohol would only be bought with the knowledge of the senior management team. We would buy no more than one bottle at a time and would set limits according to common sense.'

Other agencies would stress the carer's and the worker's rights. Should the carer have to buy alcohol which will then mean that the drinker is going to cause all sorts of problems? There are no easy answers to this question.

Arthur

'My sister Delia lives in the end house of a terrace of Tudor thatched cottages. She is 74 and has become increasingly dependent on alcohol as the years have passed. Her life has become so restricted that she eats, sleeps and baths in her front room. As I live on the other side of the country, I hadn't seen Delia for some time. However, a social worker who visited her at the request of her concerned neighbours contacted me recently. He had found that she was using a three-bar electric fire to heat the room and that as she drank she was vomiting into paper handkerchiefs which she would toss on to a growing pile around the fire. This behaviour was considered to represent a real threat to her own safety and that of the neighbours. It now looks as if some action will have to be taken to prevent this situation from continuing.'

Do you permit alcohol?

Some carers will be in a position to ban the use of alcohol completely if the person they are caring for is housebound or bedridden. The simplest way to avoid alcohol problems might seem to be to prevent any access to alcohol. If the drinker cannot have access to alcohol, then she will not be able to abuse it.

This solution is not as simple as it sounds. There is a very real danger that banning alcohol will simply drive it underground. It may force people to lie, make them take unnecessary risks to purchase alcohol or drink it secretly.

Joanna

'One of her neighbours, who came in to cook my sister's lunch every day, became so frustrated by Edith's constantly drunken state that she took her bottle of brandy and placed it out of her reach on the top of the highest wardrobe in the house. The 83-year-old woman, who had a history of brittle bones, was found later in the day balancing on a rickety chair in an effort to retrieve the drink.'

Banning alcohol may cause more problems than allowing a certain amount of open drinking. Some residential homes have even found that having bars is useful for this reason, and it is interesting to listen to their experiences. In the last ten years the number of residential homes running bars of various types has increased enormously. These bars range from a small collection of drinks kept by the staff and brought out on special occasion to a fully stocked and licensed bar.

The reason for opening the bar is not, of course, concern about alcohol problems. They are there to offer residents options that would be available to people not living in a home. The bar acts as a way of normalising the residents' life. Yet will it not cause more problems than it solves? Will it be a threat to those residents who are concerned about their drinking? Some alcohol specialists have been horrified at the prospect of allowing bars in residential homes.

The general rule in society seems to be that the more alcohol is available, the more will be drunk. The ease with which alcohol can be bought in corner shops and supermarkets seems to have increased the amount drunk in the last 20 years. More importantly, the greater the amount drunk, the greater the problems caused by alcohol. On this basis it would seem strange to support the opening of bars in residential homes. Yet a bar may be a way of controlling drinking.

Many homes that run bars have found that opening the bar encourages more sociable drinking and enables staff to monitor how much is being consumed.

Residential home manager

'We are in the process of applying for a licence because we think it can be a pleasant social activity when not taken to extremes. The benefits of the bar are the chance to be sociable, giving the residents something to look forward to, and the chance to celebrate birthdays and special occasions.'

However, none of the homes allow the bar to become a licence for drunkenness.

Residential home manager

'We limit how much residents can drink when the resident has had enough and is not able to consume anymore. Certain residents know their limits, others will just go on and on. We observe them and stop serving when aggression shows or if they are on drugs that limit consumption.'

There can be no right or wrong answer about controlling drinking. Some people will respond well to this approach and will benefit from being allowed access to alcohol in a controlled manner. Others will reject any attempt at control and may react against the restriction by drinking more.

Dealing with drunkenness

If you care for a problem drinker, she may on occasion be drunk in such a way that there is a threat either to you, the carer, or to the drinker herself. This section offers some guidance on handling these situations.

From the caring point of view it may seem useful to know how someone behaves when drunk and to know what she talks about at this time; when drunk she may begin to open up about problems and express a desire for help in a way that she never does when sober. Having such a conversation is usually a pointless exercise. Most alcohol agencies will see only people who are sober or, perhaps on a first occasion, slightly intoxicated. Some people can tolerate large amounts of alcohol, and it is possible to go through a lengthy interview with an apparently mildly intoxicated person only to find that nothing is recalled afterwards. These agencies have learned from bitter experience that an interview with an intoxicated person is usually fruitless.

There is no single way of dealing with an episode of drunkenness because the action taken will depend on the 'threat' posed by the person and the situation in which the drunken person is found.

For someone caring at home the main priority must be to protect oneself, others and the problem drinker. If the person is simply noisy and disruptive, the carer may want to leave the drinker somewhere quiet. Remember, though, it is best not to try to take the person up or down stairs in case of accidents.

Protecting the drinker

Accidents are the commonest cause of physical harm from alcohol. If a person does not show any willingness to change, carers may want to think about how to ensure she does not cause herself too much harm. If there is a danger of accident or injury, the priority will be to keep the person in a safe place until further help can be called.

A little creative thinking can produce interesting ways of tackling problems. For example, smoking while drinking in bed is a common cause of problems. Two tips have been suggested for minimising this risk:

■ Give the drinker a bucket of sand as an ashtray. It is much harder to miss a bucket than an ashtray.
■ Encourage her to smoke roll-ups which go out if not smoked.

Another possible danger is that after drinking the person may fall out of bed and break her hip. In such circumstances the carer could put her mattress on the floor to stop her rolling out of bed.

85

Protecting others

If the 'threat' is violence to the carer or to other people, the priority has to be to protect yourself and others. This will generally mean simply moving away from the drunk person in a non-threatening way. On these rare occasions when the drinker is threatening or violent, remember:

■ Women are often better at handling drunken people than men – they tend to invite less violence.

■ If things look difficult, sitting down may defuse the situation.

■ Keep exits clear – don't let the person feel penned in. The carer may want an escape route too.

■ Above all, never forget that in situations of violence or threatened violence, call the police. It is easy to play down threats of violence in a domestic setting, but there should never be any hesitation about calling the police.

8 Combining alcohol with other drugs

Alcohol is in itself a dangerous drug. However, when mixed with other drugs, even prescribed medication, its dangers are doubled. This is a particular problem for older people, who are statistically more likely to be taking both prescribed and over-the- counter medication.

This chapter looks at the main mood-altering drugs – tranquillisers, anti-depressants and the new drug Prozac – and highlights the problems associated with the use of alcohol while taking them.

Alcohol can also cause problems when combined with all sorts of other, non-mood altering-drugs, ranging from aspirins to antibiotics. This chapter lists some of the dangers.

Fiona

'I don't think that any of her friends or family realised what was going on until the day her mother fell down the stairs.'

'My friend Angela is in her late 40s. She hasn't worked since the birth of her twin children. About ten years ago her father was killed in a car crash. Her mother immediately moved into the family home and has never left, owing to her distressed condition – largely the result of drinking to cope with her terrible feelings of bereavement. Angela's mother was a tremendous burden for her, and as a result she began to drink with her mother. Her doctor had already put her on tranquillisers both to cope with her own sense of loss and to help her deal with the stress of looking after her very difficult mother; thus she was taking a cocktail of prescribed tranquillisers and alcohol.

'I don't think that any of her friends or family really realised what was going on until the day her mother fell down the stairs. Angela had been drinking on top of her tranquillisers and had passed out in her chair. Her mother had then taken a fall down the stairs, and when she couldn't wake Angela with her shouts, she had crawled to the telephone and phoned for an ambulance. They had had to break into the house and both mother and daughter had had to be taken to hospital. When Angela came round, she was as horrified as her family about what had happened, but as yet she has not been able to give up either the drinking or the tranquillisers.'

Mood-altering drugs

Many people who are experiencing problems will be prescribed mood-altering drugs by their doctor and will be using alcohol at the same time. In addition, many people who suffer problems because of their alcohol use may be prescribed mood-altering drugs to help them come off alcohol.

For a long time the main group of mood-altering drugs has been the benzodiazepine tranquillisers. These drugs are prescribed by doctors to help anxiety problems, sleeping difficulties and a number of other related issues. They first came on to the market in the 1960s to replace the more dangerous barbiturates. These were also sleeping tablets and were available under names such as Tuinal, Nembutal and Seconal. The danger with barbiturates lay in the ease with which you could overdose on them. They were especially lethal if taken with alcohol. Many of the famous rock stars who died in the sixties and seventies of drug overdoses were taking barbiturates at the time. They have been controlled under the Misuse of Drugs Act and are now much less common than they were.

As a result of these well-founded concerns, the benzodiazepine tranquillisers have replaced the barbiturates. This group of drugs includes:

- Valium (also available under its generic name diazepam);
- Librium (chlordiazepoxide);
- Ativan (lorazepam);
- Dalmane (flurazepam hydrochloride);
- Mogadon (nitrazepam)
- Hemineverin (chlormethiazole), a tranquilliser particularly used to help withdraw people from alcohol.

While these drugs are safer than barbiturates in combination with alcohol, they can still be dangerous. However, the main problem is simply that as tranquillisers they numb the emotions and greatly reduce the quality of the user's life. People who have used them often describe themselves as being like 'zombies' or living a 'half life'. Yet these drugs do have benefits – those who are suffering great emotional stress can be comforted by having their emotions dulled. On the other hand, this does mean that any good and pleasurable emotions will also be dulled. As a result they should be used only for relatively short periods of time, perhaps weeks rather than years.

Giving up tranquillisers

It is not easy to give up the use of any drug, whether it be alcohol, heroin or cigarettes. However, giving up prescribed tranquillisers can be particularly difficult. There are two main sets of reasons:

- the problems of withdrawing;
- the way they were obtained.

Surprisingly for a drug which is readily and easily prescribed by GPs, it is often said that tranquillisers are the hardest drug from which to withdraw, harder even than drugs like alcohol or heroin. Although not everyone will have problems, many long-term users will suffer severe difficulties when they give up. These can range from minor problems such as sweating, loss of appetite and anxiety through to more major problems like panic attacks, agoraphobia and suicidal feelings. These unpleasant withdrawal symptoms can last for several months. This makes it hard not to start taking the drugs again.

The second problem is that these drugs will have been prescribed by a respected member of the community – the doctor. As a result the user may feel that she ought to be taking them. She may find it hard to go to the doctor and ask to change, as this may seem to her like challenging the doctor's opinion. This is made all the worse by the fact that when the person stops taking the drugs she may experience withdrawal symptoms which mimic the anxiety state for which the drug was prescribed in the first place. This can persuade the user that she actually needed to be on the drugs after all.

As a result of these problems, tranquilliser users need to receive good advice about giving up. Their GP or a local community psychiatric nurse can help with this, and they will probably put the user on a slow-reducing programme to wean them off the drugs. In some areas tranquilliser support groups have been set up. These allow users to help one another give up. Local alcohol or drug agencies will know where the nearest group can be found.

Anybody using any of these drugs should always see their doctor before changing their medication or dosage.

Anti-depressants

Many people think that anti-depressants are the same as tranquillisers and use the terms interchangeably. They are not the same. Although both may be prescribed for people with problems of depression, they work in very different ways. Benzodiazepine tranquillisers have an immediate effect on the user's mood, just as alcohol does. Anti-depressants work slowly over a period of time to alter the body's chemical balance and thus have a positive effect on mood.

Prozac

The range of mood-altering drugs available is constantly changing. The latest and most controversial addition to the pharmacist's shelf is Prozac. Prozac is the brand name for a drug called

Fluoxetine hydrochloride. It is an anti-depressant, and has become an increasingly common choice of medication for people suffering from various forms of depression. Both users of alcohol and carers have been prescribed it to cope with the depression associated with their situations.

Prozac is different from other treatments for depression. Many users claim that it not only alleviates their depression but also gives them a lift and makes them feel more than just normal, positively well. It is also much harder to overdose on Prozac than on other anti-depressant drugs.

Prozac is a relatively new drug, so it is hard to predict whether its promise will be fulfilled or whether it will come to be regarded in the same way as Valium. Valium was meant to be a non-addictive alternative to the highly dangerous barbiturate drugs, but has turned out to have its own addictive properties.

Mixing mood-altering drugs and alcohol

Benzodiazepines, anti-depressants and Prozac all interact differently with alcohol. However, there can be no doubt that the safest advice is not to mix alcohol with any mood-altering drug. Anti-depressants can be dangerous in combination with alcohol and there are examples of people fatally overdosing with this combination. With Prozac, too, the best advice is to drink only limited amounts of alcohol or none at all.

As far as the benzodiazepines are concerned, taking alcohol on top of these drugs will increase the effect of the drugs on the user. Both drugs are depressants and in combination they will have a more powerful depressant effect. This does not make them lethal, but it can put the user at greater risk of accidents and other dangers related to loss of control over oneself.

Just as significantly, it should be remembered that prescribed drugs are given for reasons and to achieve particular medical goals. If alcohol is added to this combination, it could change the way the drugs work and prevent them doing what the doctor intended. Under the influence of alcohol, the user may also forget to take her drugs or forget that they have been taken and repeat the dose.

Other drugs

So far we have concentrated on mood-altering drugs. It is worth remembering that alcohol can have a negative effect on a whole range of other drugs. This section contains a list of interactions between alcohol and other drugs.

Drugs taken for	*When combined with alcohol*
Rheumatism/arthritis	*May cause stomach upset*
Epilepsy	*May both affect the control the drug affords and cause drowsiness*
Diabetes	*May cause headaches, skin flushes; may even lead to coma in extreme cases*
High blood pressure	*May cause dizziness/faintness if blood pressure becomes too low*
Anti-coagulants	*May cause internal bleeding*
Sleeplessness	*May worsen the natural sleeping pattern*
Painkillers	*May lead to worse problems in the long run*
Depression	*May increase the depression*
Anxiety	*May cause drowsiness*
Travel sickness	*May cause drowsiness*
General infections	*May cause headaches and flushing*

This list is not exhaustive, and it should certainly not be used as the basis for changing someone's medication without first consulting a GP. If in doubt about whether to drink when taking a particular drug or not, ask either a pharmacist or a doctor. More importantly, if someone is drinking heavily it is important that the doctor knows. Otherwise this can lead to misdiagnosis and thus inappropriate, or even dangerous, treatment.

9 Prevention

Although it will be of little comfort to those living with someone with an alcohol problem, it is still true that prevention is always better than cure. If you are concerned about someone's drinking but it is not yet a real problem, there are two main things you can do. Firstly, you can make sure that she has access to and understands the basic information about alcohol. Secondly, you can try to ensure that help and support are available at times of stress or distress which might lead to her drinking problematically. This chapter looks at these very simple ways to try to prevent problems developing.

Peter

'I was amazed when I heard how little the doctor thought it was safe to drink.'

'I live with my wife Ellen. We are both in our late 60s and are retired on reasonable pensions. We have a comfortable life and I think it's fair to say that since giving up work we have both been drinking more heavily than in the past. We enjoy having a bottle of wine at lunchtime – it makes the day pass much more smoothly – and in the evening we will have a gin or two plus a nightcap.

'It was only when I began to suffer stomach pains a few months back that I began to realise the effect that alcohol was having on me. The doctor diagnosed gastritis, which I think is an irritation of the stomach lining. She told me it was caused by drinking and proceeded to show me the safe limits. I was amazed when I heard how little the doctor thought it was safe to drink – both Ellen and I had been drinking well over those limits for some time. The doctor was very clear that we both needed to cut down and that if we didn't there might be more problems further down the line. She gave us some leaflets and the address of a local alcohol agency.

'However, Ellen and I sat down and thought very carefully about cutting down. We decided to have two drink-free days each week and are now drinking only in the evenings. At lunchtime we have soft drinks like apricot juice, which I must say makes a pleasant change. I guess we're quite grateful to the doctor for her help.'

Providing information

Most of the basic, essential information about alcohol is contained in the first two chapters of this book. Everyone in this country should understand the information about units of alcohol, the sensible drinking limits and the drink/drive laws and have a basic understanding of the effects of alcohol on the body. This is not in itself difficult. The problem comes when you try to convey this information to someone in a way that is both helpful and not threatening. You can easily imagine how pushing the facts about alcohol at someone could lead to some very curt responses.

Yet providing information is important because:

- It informs the drinker.
- It gives the drinker choices.
- It can act as a way of starting discussion on alcohol-related issues. If the opportunity presents itself, carers can sit down with the drinker and talk about the contents of, for example, an information leaflet in an informal way.

Inevitably the manner in which this information can and will be conveyed will depend very much on who you are and who your target audience is. If you are the partner of someone who you feel needs to hear this advice, your options will be very different from those open to the warden of a residential home for older people.

Ultimately the best way to impart information is to talk directly about your concerns and share the facts in that way, with the added support of a leaflet or booklet about alcohol. An alternative might be to ask some relevant professional to impart the information. However, if such a direct approach seems out of the question, then simply leaving alcohol education material lying around might be a suitable alternative. Leaflets are readily available. Your local GP's surgery or health centre will probably have leaflets; if not, then your local health promotion unit or alcohol advice centre will certainly have suitable materials. If all else fails, the national bodies listed at the back of the book will be able to furnish information. It is also quite common to find useful books about alcohol and alcohol problems in the health section of bookshops.

Information-giving for the professional carer

The professional carer has a wider range of options available. For a start educational posters can be put up in day centres, surgeries, offices and residential facilities, in a way that they cannot be displayed at home. Relevant leaflets can also be prominently presented. There are plenty of attractive health education posters and leaflets about alcohol. Such material can be displayed along with literature on local alcohol agencies. Health education units attached to the local Health Authority will have material available. Other local alcohol agencies may have produced their own leaflets. Contact them to see what is available.

However, such passive methods are always hit and miss. Those who are keen to do something could put on more specific events such as a talk on alcohol. This may seem out of place as a one-off event, but would fit well as part of a series of talks on health-related topics. In some day centres for older people the members have organised their own programme of health education to inform themselves about diet and nutrition, heating and health, and other related topics. Such age-well campaigns would provide an excellent forum for introducing messages about alcohol and health.

There are innumerable ways of getting the message about alcohol and health across. These range from talks to videos, from theatre groups to poster campaigns. Whatever the medium chosen the basic message is the same: alcohol is a vital issue and everyone must be aware of the units and limits information.

Dealing with emotional stresses

However, providing information alone will never stop alcohol problems altogether. People do not drink simply because they are ignorant of the facts; they drink because their life seems unbearable without alcohol. If we are to prevent problems, we need to be able to identify those stresses and strains which are likely to lead to someone drinking unhealthily.

Chapter 2 outlined some of the reasons why people drink. They are innumerable, but some key features do emerge. For everyone, no matter what their age, the inability to deal appropriately with emotions is a key reason for drinking.

Roger

'I used to get so frustrated at work. Everyone seemed to be dumping on me. But I've never been one to complain, so I used to take on job after job, while I could see other people sitting around chatting. It made my blood boil, and I used to bottle it all up, and then after work I would stop in at the station buffet and have two cans of strong lager. With that all the stresses seemed to disappear.'

Most of us can sympathise with the idea of using alcohol to relieve difficult emotions, but when this becomes a regular escape route it will almost certainly bring problems with it. If we want to prevent alcohol problems, one of the best ways will therefore be to help people relieve their emotions through more constructive channels such as talking about their feelings or by physical exertion.

Older people are often thought to have a stress-free life. 'They haven't got anything to do all day, so what is there to get stressed about?' seems to be a common attitude. Anyone who has watched an older person coping with isolation, boredom or physical pain will know that the stress-free image is a long way from the truth.

In particular, older people are more likely to suffer bereavements than any other group. There is little argument that losing a loved one is the greatest possible cause of emotional stress. Everyone will lose loved ones during their adult life, but older people will commonly see a string of lifelong friends dying, while at the same time facing the ever more real possibility of their own death. This is bound to be a cause of emotional stress.

Jenny

'After George died, I couldn't cope with anything any more. My friends and family seemed either too embarrassed or too uninterested to visit me, so I shut the door and took to drinking. I was 78 and rapidly becoming a drunk.'

If you want to prevent drink problems you will need to recognise that older people may need a great deal of support if they are to avoid resorting to alcohol at times of stress.

10 Caring for the carer

Alcohol does not simply harm the person who is drinking. In many ways those closest to the drinker suffer even more. The husband and wife, father or mother, son or daughter, can be as damaged by the drinking as the drinker. This chapter highlights these stresses. It emphasises the message that whatever else you do as someone caring for a problem drinker, you must make sure that you look after yourself. Looking to your own interests may be the best way of helping both you and the drinker.

The chapter also notes that these stressful relationships can lead to very abusive situations. The relationship between alcohol and the abuse of older people is also explored. While carers tend to suffer most, other people can also be affected; a grandchild may, for example, be damaged by a grandparent's drinking.

Kate

'With each fresh achievement my confidence grew, until I decided last year to take a university course. It has made a huge difference to my life.'

'At first when I started attending the counselling all I wanted to talk about was how awful Edward had been to me over the years. I couldn't see that I would need to talk about me at all. Edward is the problem not me. As the weeks went by, my counsellor gently showed me that I could not control

Edward, I could only control me. So we began to turn the attention to what I could do to find some happiness in the ghastly situation I lived in. At first going out, meeting new people, developing new interests was the last thing I wanted to do. So the first thing the counsellor did was build up my confidence and self-esteem. The years of living with a drunk had sent my sense of self-worth to absolute zero.

'Over the weeks the counsellor set me small goals to aim at, and with each fresh achievement my confidence grew, until I decided last year to take a university course. It has made a huge difference to my life.'

The carer's needs

None of the options offered earlier in the book guarantees you success. There can be no certainty that a problem drinker in your care can or will ever change. The techniques and services outlined may be your best chance for change, but sadly some people will continue to drink until it kills them. As a result it is vital that, as a carer, you spend as much time looking after yourself as you do looking after the drinker.

The drinker may be quite contented while you may spend long hours worrying, cleaning up the mess left behind, bailing her out of difficult circumstances and covering up for absences and other failures. All of this will take a huge emotional toll.

Teresa

'My husband John has drunk heavily ever since we met. After five years of marriage I began to realise that I was becoming a nobody. I spent all my life waiting around to see what state John would be in when he came back from the pub. I finally decided to spend more time on myself. I joined a couple of evening classes and began to contact old friends that I hadn't seen for ages because I hadn't wanted to go out. I am afraid that John did not change his drinking pattern at all, but I felt that at least I was getting something out of life.'

Teresa's situation is all too common. People begin to lose sight of their own needs in their concern for the drinker. This cannot be healthy and may worsen the situation. However, not everyone can change as readily as Teresa. For some people this pattern of behaviour may have lasted for 20 to 30 years. After such a time it will be no simple task to get up and go out and make a new life. Indeed, for some people, there may be real barriers to starting a new life. If John had been violent and threatening whenever Teresa had attempted to see her friends, it would have been much harder to change.

In such situations counselling and advice are essential. Your local alcohol counselling agency will be happy to offer support to the carer of a drinker and will readily give you a confidential appointment. Even if the person you care for is attending the same centre, the counsellor will not reveal to the drinker anything you say in your sessions.

Many carers will face the problem of lost confidence. The years of living with and caring for a drinker inevitably wear down self-confidence. The best advice to any carer in this situation is to seek help as soon as possible.

Problems encountered when drinking ends

The carer's problems do not cease when the drinker puts down the bottle. People who have cared for a drinker will have become used to a particular pattern of life. This may have been very difficult, but they may well have become used to taking full responsibility for the drinker and may find it very difficult to relinquish or share that role once the drinker becomes sober. Other, less obvious problems also lie in wait for the carer:

Jill

'It all seemed so unfair. I had put up with his drinking for 40 years, yet when he finally gave up after his second heart attack, everyone kept telling me how wonderful he was. Everyone seemed to have forgotten the 40 years of hell, and the huge efforts I had made to hold the household together.'

It would not be surprising if someone in this woman's situation felt resentment about the problem drinker's recovery. If the situation is to improve there must be a recognition that the carer will also need counselling and support. As pointed out in Chapter 6, help is available to carers. The point that must be emphasised now is that it is both normal and beneficial for carers to seek help. Alcohol agencies are used to dealing with such requests for help and will welcome calls from carers.

The needs of family members other than the main carer

Derek

'It only became clear many years later, when Sue was in counselling as a 40-year-old, that she had been sexually abused by her drunken grandfather when she was eight.'

Like ripples in a lake, the effects of an alcohol problem can spread far and wide. The man who dies of cirrhosis of the liver after a life of heavy drinking has clearly suffered because of his drinking. His wife, who suffered a nervous breakdown because of the stress of living with his drinking, is another obvious victim of the alcohol problem. She will need counselling, medication and perhaps even hospitalisation in the future. However, other people may well have suffered in ways which are less obvious.

The son who left home at 16 and ended up in a drug treatment unit at 23 may well have been pushed down that path by his father's drinking. The daughter who ends up marrying a man who repeats her father's abusive pattern may simply be repeating the pattern of behaviour she learned from her mother.

This is far from fanciful. There is clear evidence that children who have lived in families where one or other parent was drinking heavily are far more likely to repeat that pattern themselves in later life. Indeed, it is sadly true that alcohol problems seem to have a tendency to ricochet down the generations. Even if one generation misses out on the problem, the next may suffer the fate. It has been suggested that this is due to genetic influences.

There is clear evidence of children of problem drinkers going on to have alcohol or drug problems of their own. Equally the daughters of fathers with an alcohol problem appear to be far more likely than other women to marry a man with a drink problem, thus replicating their mothers' problems.

Most people caring for problem drinkers will focus their attention on the needs of the drinker. But the impact of alcohol on the other family members can be equally destructive, and it is important that young people realise the longer-term impact that alcohol can have on their lives. This is not to suggest that you should terrify young people about their life prospects, but that it might be wise to gently point out the dangers inherent in their situation. This may best be done by a skilled counsellor from an alcohol agency. See Chapter 6 on agencies that exist to provide support to carers and other members of drinkers' families.

The needs of non-family carers

Many people who care for problem drinkers, especially older problem drinkers, are not immediate family. Some will be neighbours and friends; others will be paid workers, perhaps a home carer or the warden of a residential home. These people are also carers and may be in just as much need of support as a family member. One female care worker described working with a group of older male problem drinkers as being like 'a form of abuse'.

It should not be forgotten that paid carers will also experience stress. Nor should paid staff feel ashamed about admitting their need for support and help in working with drinkers. Alcohol agencies will be happy to provide support to paid workers, but perhaps in the first instance such staff should seek help from their line managers or colleagues.

The abuse of older people

At times the emotional abuse inflicted on the carer by the drinker will be worsened by physical abuse. There is a clear link between the use of alcohol by a male partner and abuse of his wife or girlfriend. It is well known that the physical abuse of children is linked to the abuse of alcohol.

What is less often recognised is that older drinkers may also be the victims of such violence. Among older people the relationship between alcohol and abuse can be dramatically turned on its head. The drinker places herself in a very vulnerable position. She is likely to be physically less able than her carer and her irritating behaviour may goad the carer beyond endurance, leading to the physical abuse.

Anne

'My sister had lived with our mother since Judith's marriage had broken up some 15 years previously. I first realised that something was wrong when my mother broke her arm falling down stairs. When the doctor examined her he noticed a number of other bruises which were not consistent with her fall. To my horror he suggested that she was being physically abused, probably by Judith. A social worker became involved and he quickly ascertained that my mother had been drinking heavily for some time. Whenever she got drunk she would start to criticise Judith, laughing at her for not having remarried and never having had any children. Ultimately, this became too much for Judith and she hit out at mother. On one occasion she had knocked her down the stairs.'

In recent years there has been growing concern about the physical and emotional abuse of older people, and it is interesting to note that more than one commentator has suggested that the factors most significantly associated with abuse were the amount of alcohol drunk by the carer and abusive behaviour by the dependant.

One study goes so far as to suggest that 63 per cent of abusers may have a history of alcohol or drug addiction. Another case study will highlight the problems presented:

Jane

'A 72-year-old woman who suffered from moderate dementia lived with her alcoholic daughter Jane, who was a nurse. Jane became very frustrated and angry with her mother, who criticised her constantly, especially for her alcohol and drug abuse. Jane confined the mother to bed, refusing her food and drink, until she weighed four stone. This occurred on three occasions, on each of which urgent hospitalisation was required to save the woman's life because of malnutrition. She now has carer support and day hospital care. Even now she will eat little and has become an elderly anorexic.'

One study goes further and suggests that a history of alcohol abuse is a characteristic of both abuser and abused. You can readily imagine how the use of alcohol in the stressful carer–older person relationship can inflame a situation.

Useful addresses

Action on Elder Abuse
Aims to prevent abuse of older people by raising awareness, education, promoting research and the collection and dissemination of information. Action on Elder Abuse operates the Elder Abuse Response, which is a confidential helpline service providing information for anyone and emotional support for those involved.

Astral House
1268 London Road
London SW16 4ER
Tel: 0181-764 7648;
Elder Abuse Response:
0800 7314141
10am-4.30pm (weekdays)

ACOA (Adult Children of Alcoholics)
Helps adults whose childhoods were badly affected by their parents' drinking.
(Please send sae.)

PO BOX 1576
London SW3 2XB
Tel: 0171-229 4587

Alcohol Concern
The national agency on alcohol misuse. It has a wide range of information and can also advise on training courses on working with problem drinkers. It can put people worried about their own or a relative's drinking in touch with a local agency.

Waterbridge House
32 Loman Street
London SE1 0EE
Tel: 0171-928 7377

Alcoholics Anonymous (AA)
A self-help group for problem drinkers. Members attend regular group meetings and renounce alcohol for life.

PO Box 1
Stonebow House
Stonebow
York YO1 2NJ
Tel: 01904 644026

Al-Anon Family Groups UK and Eire
Offers understanding and support for families and friends of problem drinkers.

61 Great Dover Street
London SE1 4YF
Tel: 0171-403 0888
(24 hour confidential helpline)

Alateen
A part of Al-Anon, is for young people aged 12-20 who have been affected by someone else's drinking, usually that of a parent.

61 Great Dover Street
London SE1 4YF
Tel: 0171-403 0888

Drinkline
A confidential helpline offering advice, support and information to anyone concerned about their own drinking or that of a friend or relative.

Tel: 0345 32 02 02
Mon-Friday 11am-11pm
0500 801 802
(24-hour dial and listen)

Medical Council on Alcoholism
Agency concerned with the medical care of problem drinkers.

3 St Andrews Place
London NW1 4LB
Tel: 0171-487 4445

The Portman Group
A drinks industry-funded group; produces educational materials and supports research on alcohol-related matters.

2A Wimpole Street
London W1M 7AA
Tel: 0171-499 1010

Further reading

'Abuse of Elderly People by their Carers' (1990) A Homer and C Gilleard, *British Medical Journal* Vol 301, 15 Dec 1990, pp 1359–1362.

Alcohol and the Black Communities (undated) G Nolan and C Day, DAWN.

Alcohol and Public Health (1991) Royal College of General Practitioners.

Alcohol Awareness: Towards a transcultural approach (1990) Alcohol Training Project.

Alcohol Our Favourite Drug (1987) Royal College of Psychiatrists, Tavistock.

Alcohol Problems in Old Age (1995) M Ward and C Goodman, Wynne Howard Books.

Alcohol Services Directory (1995) Alcohol Concern.

Counselling for Alcohol Problems (1992) R Velleman, Sage.

The Demon Drink (1988) J Robinson, Methuen.

Drinking in England and Wales in the Late 1980s (1991) E Goddard, HMSO.

A Great and Growing Evil (1987) Royal College of Physicians, Tavistock.

Problem Drinking: The new approach (1989) N Heather and I Robertson, Oxford Medical Publications.

Say When! Everything a woman needs to know about alcohol (1989) R Kent, Sheldon Press.

Teaching about Alcohol Problems (1987) Alcohol Concern.

The Treatment of Drinking Problems (1982) G Edwards, Grant MacIntyre.

Women and Alcohol (1980) Camberwell Council on Alcoholism, Tavistock.

Women under the Influence (1991) B McConville, Grafton Books.

About Age Concern

Caring for someone with an alcohol problem is one of a wide range of publications produced by Age Concern England, the National Council on Ageing. Age Concern cares about all older people and believes later life should be fulfilling and enjoyable. For too many this is impossible. As the leading charitable movement in the UK concerned with ageing and older people, Age Concern finds effective ways to change that situation.

Where possible, we enable older people to solve problems themselves, providing as much or as little support as they need. Our network of 1,400 local groups, supported by 250,000 volunteers, provides community-based services such as lunch clubs, day centres and home visiting.

Nationally, we take a lead role campaigning, parliamentary work, policy analysis, research, specialist information and advice provision, and publishing. Innovative programmes promote healthier lifestyles and provide older people with opportunities to give the experience of a lifetime back to their communities.

Age Concern is dependent on donations, covenants and legacies.

Age Concern England
1268 London Road
London SW16 4ER
Tel: 0181-679 8000

Age Concern Scotland
113 Rose Street
Edinburgh EH2 3DT
Tel: 0131-220 3345

Age Concern Cymru
4th Floor
1 Cathedral Road
Cardiff CF1 9SD
Tel: 01222 371566

Age Concern Northern Ireland
3 Lower Crescent
Belfast BT7 1NR
Tel: 01232 245729

Other books in this series

Choices for the carer of an elderly relative
Marina Lewycka
Being a carer may mean many different things – from living at a distance and keeping a check on things by telephone to taking on a full-time caring role. This book looks at the choices facing someone whose parent or other relative needs care. It helps readers to look at their own circumstances and their own priorities and decide what is the best role for themselves – as well as the person being cared for.
£6.99 0-86242-263-9

Caring for someone who has dementia
Jane Brotchie
Caring for someone with dementia can be physically and emotionally exhausting, and it is often difficult to think about what can be done to make the situation easier. This book shows how to cope better and seek further help as well as containing detailed information on the illness itself and what to expect in the future.
£6.99 0-86242-259-0

Caring for someone who has had a stoke
Philip Coyne with Penny Mares
Supportive and positive, this book is designed to help carers understand stroke and its immediate aftermath and contains extensive information on hospital discharge, providing care, rehabilitation and adjustment to life at home.
£6.99 0-86242-264-7

Caring for someone who is dying
Penny Mares
Confronting the knowledge that a loved one is going to die soon is always a moment of crisis. And the pain of the news can be

compounded by the need to take responsibility for the care and support given in the last months and weeks. This book attempts to help readers cope with their emotions, identify the needs which the situation creates and make the practical arrangements necessary to ensure that the passage through the period is as smooth as possible.

£6.99 0-86242-260-4

Going home from hospital
Sheila White

The impending arrival of an older person home after a period in hospital commonly puts family members under significant strain. Often existing living arrangements have to be reorganised and additional care responsibilities shouldered. This book offers advice on the practical planning necessary and highlights sources of help and support.

£6.99 0-86242-155-1

The carer's handbook: What to do and who to turn to
Marina Lewycka

At some point in their lives millions of people find themselves suddenly responsible for organising the care of an older person with a health crisis. All too often such carers have no idea what services are available or who can be approached for support. This book is designed to act as a first point of reference in just such an emergency, signposting readers on to many more detailed, local sources of advice.

£6.99 0-86242-262-0

Finding and paying for residential and nursing home care
Marina Lewycka

Acknowledging that an older person needs residential care often represents a major crisis for family and friends. Feelings of guilt and betrayal invariably compound the difficulties faced in identifying a suitable care home and sorting out the financial arrangements. This book provides a practical step-by-step guide to the decisions which have to be made and the help which is available.

£6.99 0-86242-261-2

Publications from Age Concern Books

Money matters

Your Rights: A guide to money benefits for older people
Sally West

In clear and concise language, Your Rights guides readers through the maze of money benefits for older people and explains what you can claim and why. Specific sections are provided on: Retirement Pensions; Housing and Council Tax Benefit; benefits for disabled people; Income Support and the Social Fund; paying for residential care; help with legal and health costs.

For further information please ring 0181–679 8000.

Health and care

The Community Care Handbook: The reformed system explained (2nd edition)
Barbara Meredith

The provision of care in the community is changing as a result of recent legislation. Written by one of the country's foremost experts, this book explains in practical terms the background to the reforms, what they are, how they are working and who they affect.

£13.99 0-86242-171-3

If you would like to order any of these titles, please write to the address below, enclosing a cheque or money order for the appropriate amount made payable to Age Concern England. Credit card orders may be made on 0181-679 8000.

Mail Order Unit, Age Concern England, 1268 London Road London SW16 4ER

Factsheets from Age Concern

Covering many areas of concern to older people, Age Concern's factsheets are comprehensive and totally up to date. There are over 40 factsheets, with each one providing straightforward information and impartial advice in a simple and easy-to-use format. Topics covered include:

- finding and paying for residential and nursing home care
- raising income from your home
- money benefits
- legal arrangements for managing financial affairs
- finding help at home

Single copies are available free on receipt of a 9" × 12" sae.

Age Concern offers a factsheet subscription service which presents all the factsheets in a folder, together with regular updates throughout the year. The first year's subscription currently costs £40; an annual renewal thereafter is £20.

For further information, or to order factsheets, write to:

Information and Policy Division
Age Concern England
1268 London Road
London SW16 4ER

For readers in Scotland wishing further information, or to order factsheets, please write to:

Age Concern Scotland
113 Rose Street
Edinburgh EH2 3DT

Subscribers in Scotland will be automatically sent Scottish editions of factsheets where law and practice differ in Scotland.

Index

Personal Drink Diary

Day	Time	Where/ With whom	Type of drink	No of units
Mon				
Tue				
Wed				
Thu				
Fri				
Sat				
Sun				
		Total units for week		

Good and bad things about my drinking

Good	Bad
	1
	2
	3
	4
	5
	6
	7
	8
	9
	10
	11

Now ask yourself: Do I want to change my drinking?   Yes/No

Situations in which I find it hard or easy to avoid drinking

Hard to avoid drinking	Easy to avoid drinking
	1
	2
	3
	4
	5
	6
	7
	8
	9

Now ask yourself: Can I spend more time in the easy situations and less time in the hard situations?

What are the alternatives to drinking?

In this space write down what alternatives there are to drinking, what you could do instead of drinking

Now ask yourself: Which of these will I try?

Targets I will work towards

How many units will I drink this week?

What else will I change about my life? (be specific)

How will I reward myself if I reach these targets?

Why I didn't succeed	How I can improve on this next time